southbound DPU

January 2011

Eugene, OR- It's been one of those days when you keep waiting for something to happen but nothing ever does. I have a girl-from-Nebraska's car and she was supposed to be back three days ago but I haven't heard from her since December and I now need to leave town, I'm waiting for Tone to call me back about the sudden death of a mutual friend whose house I have stayed at many-a-times and I don't want to over-speculate about something as serious based on what I've second-hand heard, and I've been trying desperately to get in touch with Oregon's DHS office in town or in Portland but can't get through and I have been waiting for the fourth of this month since at least Christmastime for my food-stamps. The only one who has responded is my mother, who just had her knee operated on.

A train went south from the yard around 0730 with no DPU, only a Freddy, so I didn't bother catching it. Around 1030 a six-unit general manifest pulled in from the south sporting one newly painted Western Pacific Feather River Route engine that had railfans chasing it across town. One young super-foamer came peddling down under Chambers on a tweeker-bike wearing a brand new Southern Pacific Lines-jacket with a walkie-talkie tuned in to the yard's frequency tucked into the pocket.

"This one's three hours late," he told me of the dripping train. "It was supposed to be here at six this morning."

After trying to sell him a zine I sent him down the Northwest Hwy to inspect the departure tracks for me. He never reported back. Less than an hour later another northbound blew by on the mainline—mostly Canadian cars (big-belly grainers, BCOLs, WCs, SRYs, etc.)—and pulled all the way down to Beltline to CC. Minutes later headlights beamed on in the yard and a southbound pulled

-Chambers Bridge-

slowly out toward me, a three-unit general manifest with boxcars closed and sealed and lumber loaded and stenciled BANKS OREGON (a small lumber town in the Coast Range outside of Portland). I waited for the engines to pass under Chambers then stood on the other side of the middle bridge-pillar. There was no stopping at Van Buren to switch tracks, the train moved right on through and I caught the rear unit on the fly at about 6 mph, hustled up the steps, and ran down the walkway to the cab before being exposed to cars driving by. The train passed unsteadily through Eugene, slowed toward Judkins, and stopped dead on the mainline, where across the river through the barren trees I could make out the large yellow O of Autzen Stadium. (I always get nervous when the DPU unexpectedly stops, especially on the mainline, and especially when still in town. I worry about being pulled off before ever leaving) . . . *As far as I am aware, only one person has spotted me in the DPU and that was a tramp sitting under the highway in Washington-Jefferson Park, and he waved. But even if anyone else did see me, they probably wouldn't know I am not supposed to be here. Still, I'm not relaxing until out of Eugene . . .*

Piles of burnettized ties lay every ten or so yards along the mainline, signs of track replacement to come, and inside the cab the radio was tuned in to what sounded like communication between my train and the Yardmaster in Eugene. A Brotherhood of Locomotive Engineers "Teamsters" sticker had been plastered above the dash where it was also written: Powered by Dutch Bros., which is an Oregon-based drive-thru-coffee chain. Nowhere inside the warm DPU is there a drop of water . . . *I have again shot myself in the foot by only bringing half a bottle of water, and I may have to get off in either K-Falls or Dunsmuir to refill, then wait for another southbound to come through . . .*

After five minutes the train moved slowly through Judkins siding, past Springfield Junction where the older Siskiyou line veers off on a more-westernly route south, and across the muddy (this time of year) Willamette River into Springfield. The train blared through a well-stuffed yard there, past onlooking workers at Rosboro Lumber, and onto the Natron Cutoff, which derives its name from Natron, which used to be a small station east of Springfield where several lumber mills operated and which got its name from the mineral Natrolite, found abundantly on the western slopes of the Cascade Mountains here.

Completed in 1926, the Natron Cutoff replaced the 19th-century Siskiyou line as the major freight artery between California and the lumber-rich Pacific Northwest. The cutoff saved 25 miles of track and lessened the mean-grade by an entire percent by looping along the mountainside in an S shape to gain elevation at

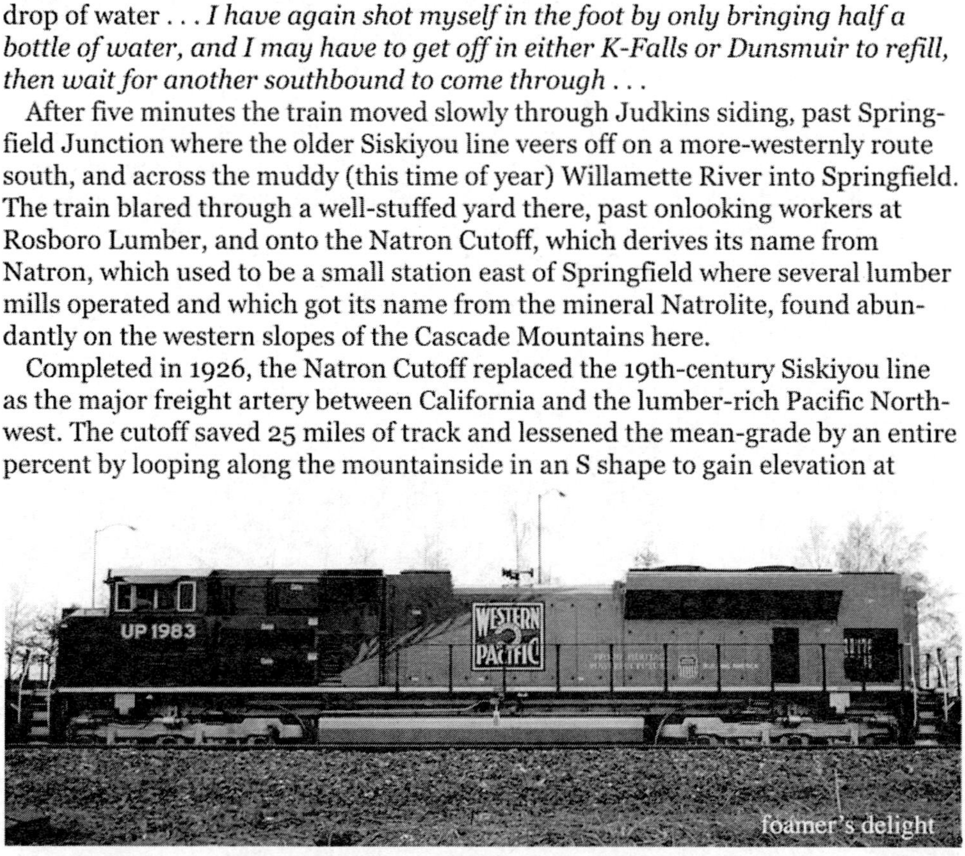

foamer's delight

more-manageable grades. The further-west Siskiyou line, generally much steeper, longer, and more curvaceous, has since been compromised considerably and today, operated by Central Oregon and Pacific (CORP), goes only as far as Medford and Ashland and no longer crosses into California.

Creaking past old dairy farms and lumber mills, the train headed endlessly toward the horizon, trudging up into the mountains, eventually becoming level with clouds that hung low in the hills. Fifty-miles from Eugene, at Minnow, a wide dam held back dwindling Dexter Reservoir, hundreds of feet low, its shores looking like a mountainside removal project with patches of trees stranded like a flat-top haircut above stripped, red mud shores. There was no snow on the ground, yet snowcaps loomed almost invisibly against the bright horizon ahead where the contours of the lake vanished. At higher elevations where the lake is lower, water draining from the mountains has carved a course of empty red crevices and the bottom islands between them are covered with short, vibrant green moss.

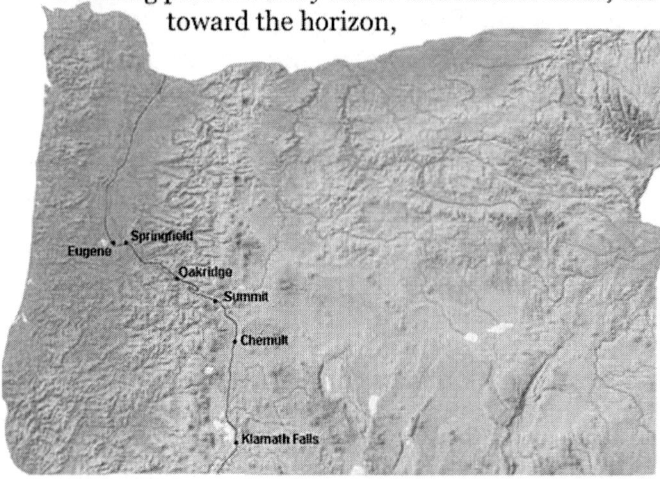

Several short tunnels later the train emerged in Oakridge. *Ohhh boy,* I thought as it pulled onto the siding. But it was only some mainline work that detoured us, and the train proceeded to leave behind Oakridge's yard of unused lumber cars. Just past Oakridge the first showing of snow appeared shoveled up alongside the roads and track-bed, as well as on the forest floor, still thawing. Here, the real climb begins: 44 miles of 1.8%-grade track.

"Amtrak 14 on the mainline. Highball at Cruzette. Over," squalks the radio.

"I'd like to pull onto Heather and work on a couple of frogs if I could. Over," the Conductor says . . .

Several miles later, as the train pulled onto a snowy siding high in the Cascades, I wondered if that indeed had been my train's Conductor communicating. Sure enough, the train stopped and I ate the snow on the ground at Heather to save water. Whatever "frogs" the Conductor was talking about I never heard croak, and after Amtrak blew north on the main-

Dexter Lake low

line, my train inched onward south.

Just after Heather, the train crossed the Salt Creek Trestle high above Hwy 58 on a westward arching curve connecting mountains of Douglas firs. Here begins the Cascade Loops, a section of track that winds back and forth to ease the steep climb up the mountains. At the base of the Loops the train passes through a section where the forest has been wiped out by what looks to be a clear-cut. This section of track—between Heather and Wicopee—is directly located 900-feet below Frazier, which was wiped out a few years back by a massive landslide; and that landslide caused a secondary landslide that avalanched all the way down the mountain to obliterate this section of track too.

The radio suddenly comes back in and I hear the Conductor communicating with dispatchers again, asking if the train can have an extra 25-minutes to make it to Abernathy and make up for some lost time. Short tunnels begin passing the train through the mountains and as elevation increases so does snow-depth, from a couple of thawing inches at Heather to almost a foot of snow at Frazier.

It is here at Frazier, on a mountain called Coyote, that a massive 20-acre landslide obliterated UP's mainline three-years ago this month. I have passed through here before, both prior to and after the landslide, but now, looking out overtop a string of gondolas and seeing off both sides of the train, I am for the first time able to see in context this cataclysm. Much of the mountain has been entirely rebuilt with complex drainage lines installed, but you wouldn't know that just by looking at it. Today it is but a barren, snow-covered mountainside, terraced in some areas of the downslope for stability, and with a slide-fence protecting the north side of the tracks from the unstable earth. The wiped out area opens up a panoramic vista across the Salt Creek Canyon—a rare view of the Cascades once obstructed by tall strands of western hemlocks and Douglas firs.

Frazier Slide site

Late in January of 2008, after a record snowfall in the Oregon Cascades—160% of normal accumulation—residents of tiny Oakridge heard a thundering explosion deep off into the night that seemed to linger in the air, then trail away. Meanwhile, Union Pacific dispatchers in Omaha Nebraska noticed they had lost CTC signals on the Cascades line and halted all trains. From Oakridge, an inspection-truck drove the rails north and arrived at milepost 561.5, the lower mainline sec-

UNION PACIFIC VS. THE MUDSLIDE

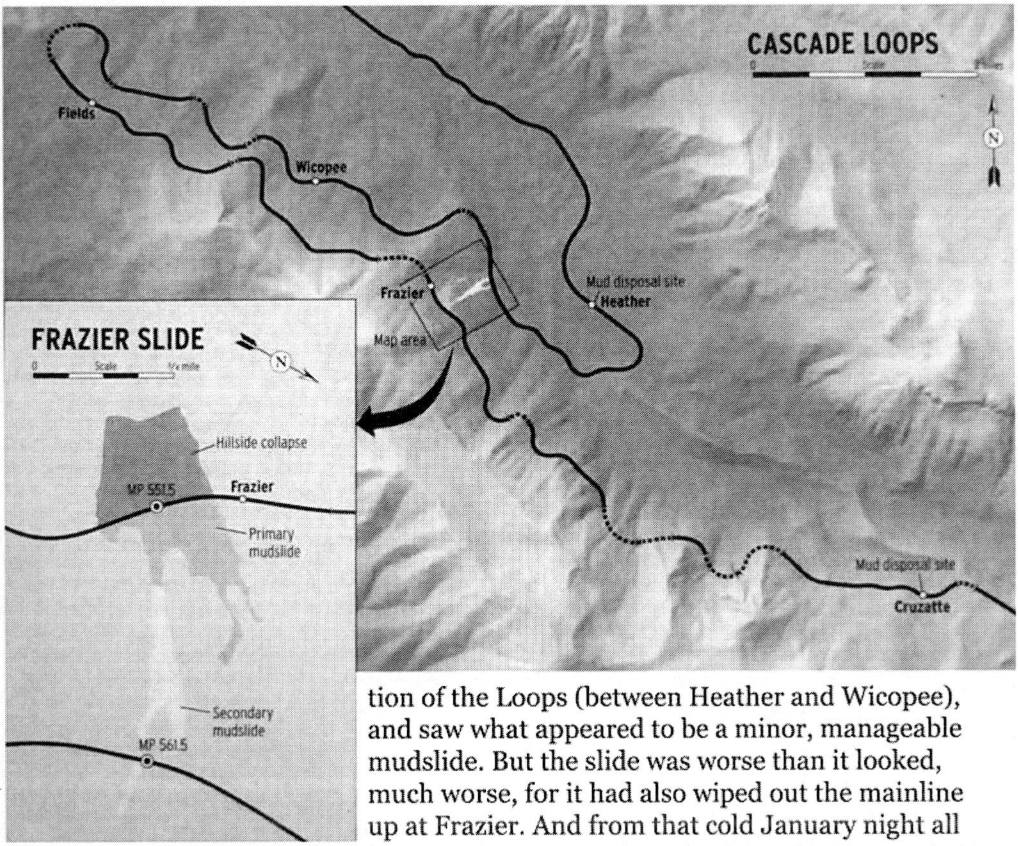

tion of the Loops (between Heather and Wicopee), and saw what appeared to be a minor, manageable mudslide. But the slide was worse than it looked, much worse, for it had also wiped out the mainline up at Frazier. And from that cold January night all the way through to early April the tracks became impassable to all trains, including bidaily Amtraks. And with the Siskiyou line not in suitable condition to handle any such volume of freight, this became an enormous problem for UP.

The slide proved so massive that trees left standing at the base of Coyote Mountain reported mud-lines on their limb-sheered trunks as much as 50-feet high. 1,500-feet of mainline track had to be rebuilt at Frazier, 700,000 board-feet of uprooted timber relocated, and 19-million cubic feet of mud removed on top of the constant plowing and shoveling of snow that at times fell hard enough to keep construction crews at bay. Not to mention that tons and tons of ballast had to be freighted in from Eugene to fill-in the hillside. Mainline traffic on the Cascades line became utterly nonexistent as the Eugene yard thinned considerably in stock and the Departure Tracks underneath Maxwell Bridge and Beltline became a temporary rock quarry where side-dump ballast cars sat in short lines, constantly being filled from five-foot-high piles of rock that had been dumped along the tracks to be sent up into the mountains to stabilize the site. Traffic was all screwed up. The normal 5 - 10 trains UP runs daily over the Cascades all had to be rerouted, some as far away as Salt Lake City via Roseville. But most trains were sent to Oregon Trunk Junction through the Deschutes River Canyon, necessitating that Union Pacific activate its trackage rights agreement with BNSF for the first time since 1907 when the Oregon Trunk subdivision was first completed amid fierce competition (see *Railroad Semantics #2*). Shipping dates for all Willamette Valley industries were significantly delayed as trains loaded in and around

Eugene had to travel all the way back up to Portland, then across to Eastern Oregon for the alternative route south. For 105-days straight, nearly twenty-four hours a day, Oakridge boomed akin to the days of steam. Restaurants were packed, hotels were full, and the bars bustled until early April 2008 when the line finally reopened to limited freight traffic and things went back to their slow way.

Frazier Slide near Oakridge, OR
January 19, 2008

Frazier to Cruzatte—five miles of hard mountain railroading involving tunnels, curving trestles, and rock sheds clinging to steep cliffs offering countless vistas and 180-degree panoramas across the canyon—is the most visually striking portion of the Cascade sub. The train plunged into two-consecutive tunnels connected by a concrete rock shed then crossed Noisy Creek Bridge, a short arched trestle leading directly into a third blackened tunnel, longer than the previous two and also with a rock shed on the end. After a brief break in mountain gaps, a fourth tunnel was passed through to reach another high curving trestle: Shady Creek Bridge, which spans to a fifth tunnel, this one 3,100-feet in length, longer than all the previous four tunnels combined. Two feet of snow sat atop signal boxes, the air smoky with exhaust, and another view across the mountains opened up just before the train entered one more short tunnel and exited onto Cruzatte, a siding carved high into the side of Judd Mountain.

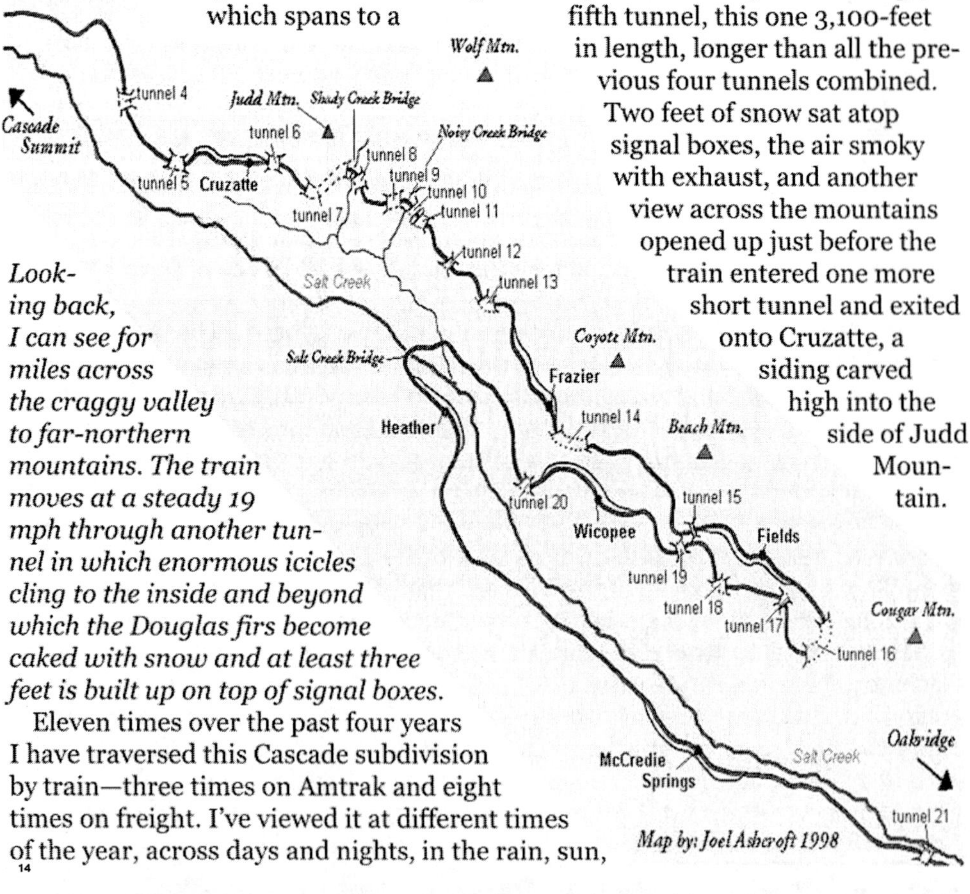

Map by: Joel Ashcroft 1998

Looking back, I can see for miles across the craggy valley to far-northern mountains. The train moves at a steady 19 mph through another tunnel in which enormous icicles cling to the inside and beyond which the Douglas firs become caked with snow and at least three feet is built up on top of signal boxes.

Eleven times over the past four years I have traversed this Cascade subdivision by train—three times on Amtrak and eight times on freight. I've viewed it at different times of the year, across days and nights, in the rain, sun, and snow; I've watched the sun set and rise over the mountains sweltering in summer heat and in freezing enough to see my breath; I've viewed it from hopper porches and out boxcar doors, from under the wheels of a semi-trailer, from the Conductor's chair inside the rear-unit, and in the headlights of the lead engine; I've crossed the pass in violent thunderstorm and I once trekked upwards of 10 miles of track one night on foot when stranded south of Oakridge. The Oregon Cascades are always a grand sight, but winter is the most beautiful time of year to see them.

Odell Lake

Radio communication suddenly interrupts, alerting me that at Crescent Lake a sidetracked northbound is to give my train a visual roll-by . . . Twenty-years ago I would have been toast because pushers used to run only up to Crescent Lake and there be broken off and turned back around to Eugene. In fact, Crescent Lake existed as a crew-change point between Eugene and Klamath Falls until 1976 and once had an engine house along with a station, clubhouse, and crew quarters. But today nothing remains and Crescent Lake is just another siding on the Cascade sub.

"UP 5383 south. Over." . . . [That's my train]

I peeked up over the top of the window at the sidetracked train and the Conductor standing by with radio in hand.

"Train 5383 south. Lookin' good boys. Highball."

"Highball."

"Go Ducks!"

"Quack. Quack." . . .

And highball we did, passing Crescent Lake at 43 mph, undeterred by all the ice and snow, gliding on silver slivers of rail emerging from a plain of pure white. The higher the elevation the bigger the sky became, and with the earth wide, flat, and uniformly colorloess, the trees became shorter and of thinner girth. BNSF's

-southbound in the Oregon Cascades Jan. 2011-

tracks merged seamlessly with UP's at Chemult, a tiny station on the east side of the Cascades along Hwy 97.

"UP detector—milepost—five—zero—one—point—zero," an automated voice monotones over the radio. "UP detector—milepost—five—zero—one—point—zero. No defects. Axel count: two—hundred—fifty—six. Miles per hour: fifty. Temperature: thirty—degrees. Detector out." . . .

Somewhere around Chiloquin it occurred to me that at Heather siding (Heather was the only place I got out and walked around) I lost my phone. After all the mishaps I've had traveling this past year, I had found yet another way to impair myself. It must've fallen out of my camera bag at some point when I was taking photos. After packing and unpacking everything twice I considered getting off in Klamath Falls altogether and going back to Eugene . . . *But really, how appropriate is my loss . . . I've been frustrated that no one is getting in touch with me when I need them to and was sick of looking at that damn phone and being reliant on it, so it's actually a little liberating to be void of it, though I really can't believe my bum luck . . .*

I stood on the back of the unit at dusk as it barreled through snowy sub-alpine forest on a slightly curving stretch of track mirroring the Williamson River, a deep gulch of snowy rocks that levels out to feed Upper Klamath Lake, which if I were not there to see for myself I would not have believed had frozen over entirely! The train stopped briefly beside the Lake to allow a northbound BNSF to pass, and I stared out across the flat desert of snow spanning to the Klamath Mountains in the west.

The train stopped to change crews in K-Falls and I stepped out onto a low bridge over a canal of high water. Minutes later I climbed back into the unit and the train pulled through the yard and headed across the snowy Klamath Basin toward glaciated Mt. Shasta on the Black Butte subdivision—110-miles of climb

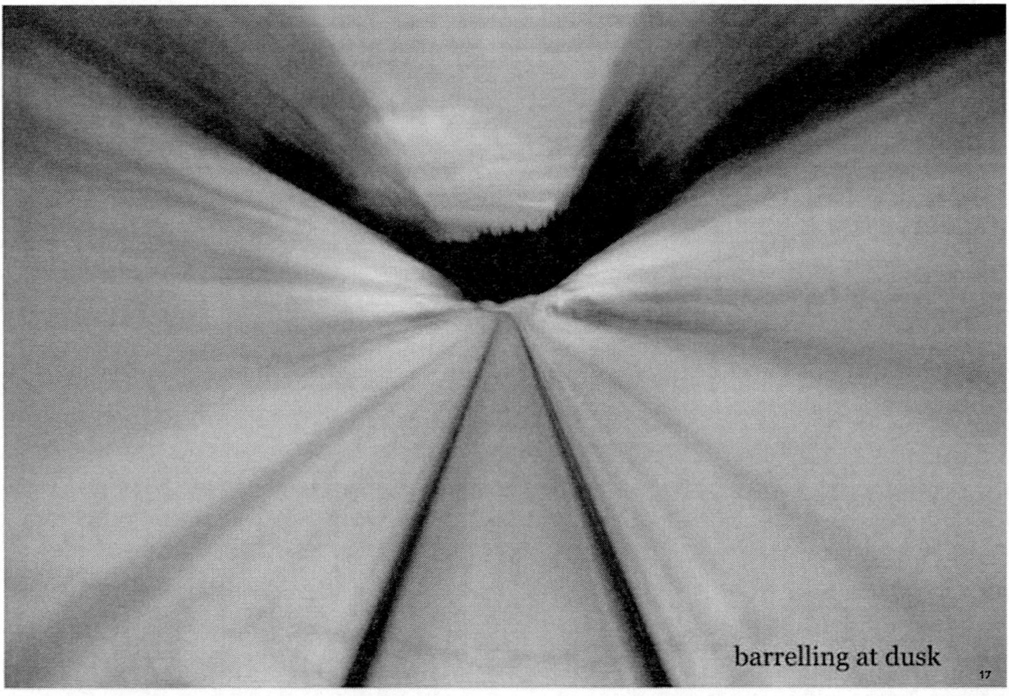

barrelling at dusk

and descent across the base of a mystic volcano.

The train stopped to change crews again in Dunsmuir several hours later and I drank my last gulp of water and stumbled out into the dark starry night. There was no snow on the ground so I tried to feel my way down to the Sacramento to fill up on water. I would have drunk from the river but just as soon the train began to move again. I considered staying there in Dunsmuir, hanging out in the Amtrak station where it's warm, hydrating myself, finding some beer perhaps, and maybe even waiting a day to meet up with T-Box, who should be on his way down for the same reason. But I didn't know what time it was, and with no phone to reach him I decided to lie back down in the cab and hope to make good time to Roseville . . . *I've been a fool to this before, and here I am embarking on another two-hundred-plus-miles dehydrating in a sweltering DPU without a drop of water . . . and it's like a placebo effect when you start to think about the stress of having no relief for thirst—the mouth seems to dry out even more . . . and although I'm lying on the floor of this unit in much better condition than last summer when I rode into Roseville with no food or water and in serious physical pain with a broken ankle, I feel almost equally in duress . . .*

I slept on and off uncomfortably with hydration on the forefront of my mind, waking time after time to thoughts of drinking water only to quickly realize I had none. But good time I made. I awoke to the train slowing along a level straightaway of track bordering industrial lots and storage units, soon a familiar arched bridge emerged from the night fog and came into view and I packed up my bag as the train worked its way into Roseville's Davis yard. I caught-off the same way I caught-on—on the fly—then walked across the yard to an industrial holding area bordering Vernon Street that for the past year has held several strings of inactive units. *I'll camp out in one until sunrise,* I thought, *sleep some more.* The very first unit I walked into was already occupied and a dark, shiny sleeping bag stirred and a guy poked his scruffy head out to look at me. "Sorry," I said. "Nevermind." The second unit I came to smelled like sanitizing chemicals and I saw the door to the lavatory open and toilet paper strewn across the floor, so I didn't sleep there. The third unit I merely looked inside of to see a tarp strung up like it was going to rain in there. It was on a different string of units entirely that I found a stone-cold, empty engine to sleep in that was still stocked with ice-cold bottles of water. Hail Mary!

foggy a.m. in Roseville

Roseville, CA- I slept hard and woke to a cold gray day across the yard. I crossed Vernon Street to look for a pay phone, and seeing a crushed coffee cup on the ground I stopped to ask a man standing in a doorway where a place to get a cup might be . . . *I've had bad luck trying to find one before, and there's no way I'm going back into Historic Roseville because I know there's nothing there . . .*

"Are you looking for something to eat?" the man asked.

"Well... ya," I responded, surprised that someone in Roseville was actually being helpful.

He pointed me in the direction of the local Salvation Army. "We're feeding right now. If you hurry, you can make it."

"Thanks," I said, looking up and seeing that I had stopped directly in front of the St. Vinnie's on Vernon St. The man must have worked there.

"We're feeding here, but not until two-thirty. Come back by then," he said.

I made it to the Sally's ok, but just as Fate's goodwill had sent me there, Karma shut the door in my face. One home-bum outside stuffed two whole Rice Crispy treats into his mouth, got on his tweeker-bike, and peddled off in first gear. Another slob smoked a post-free-breakfast cigarette, waddling back and forth on the sidewalk like an invalid. I could see all sorts of other home-bums hunched over tables inside eating, as volunteers washed dishes in the window in front of me, but I was one-hundred and twenty seconds too late. My next stop, the library, didn't open for another two hours, so I gave up on Roseville and walked the entire stretch of the yard south—a multi-mile hike.

"Hey! Need a bottle?" some scrawny brat on a stunt bike teased me as I trudged down the street. "Heee loooks depressed. I think heee neeeeds a bottle," he chimed to his three friends with an ignorant laugh. (*So this is how today's kids mock the homeless... as alcoholics?*) I just smiled and nodded my head know-

Roseville Yard Schematic Rendering

Roseville, California

- 780 Acres
- 6 Miles Long
- 136 Miles of Track
- 338 Turnouts
- 1785 Cars Switched Daily
- 600 Locomotives Repaired Monthly
- 2350 Locomotives Services Monthly
- 2,350,000 Gallons of Fuel Dispensed Monthly

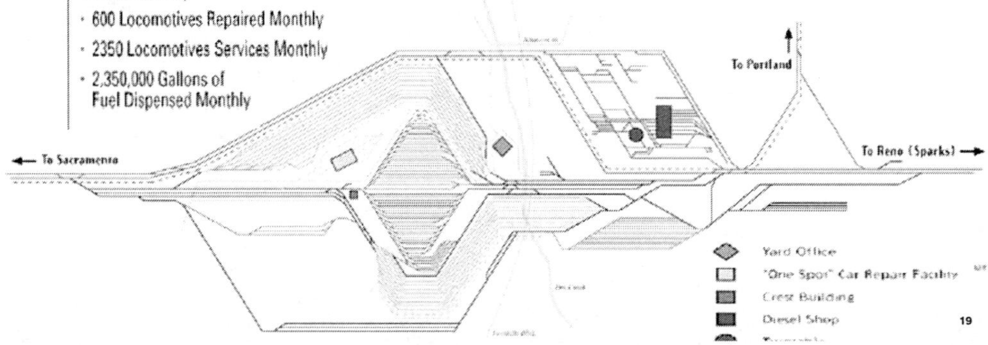

CP RV102 ANTELOPE

still Rollin
Dirty
NBD
11-10
9/16
you talk, you try!
Are you A Monster
are you A Bo, A Pro!
A Fiend, or Friend
New Times, New Rulz
New Crew
SAME GAME
We Rule
the Kingdom
of
Nigh!
12/10
BOOK 'EM
DAN'O
O.B.C.
NEVER STOP
ROCKIN
SKROZ
SCROWZ
768332
10-10
NBD
PHLP
If I don't see you,
Im headin to Portland.
-Masshole Jeff
11/10
S
J
E-VILLE
11/10
PDX
NBD
LUCKY
DOES
12.19.10
BE BACK
SHORTLY
NBD
S
F
F
S BD
10-10
GOIN
EVERYWHERE!
YES I AM
ASSHOLE
FUCK
YOU
"10"
10
SBD
FREE
Therapy
SCROWZ
PHLEM

ing that I was at least as much of a sociologically unconscious brat when I was his age (and that I was going to punch his face if he came back around).

I reached Citrus Heights, another technoburban mess of concrete, stoplights, upper-middle class enterprises, coffee-shop chains, gas stations, and big-box department stores, and I had just sat down to a corporate cup and began to write when a middle-age, middle-class white woman with two children of different ethnicity (but whom I otherwise did not notice), walked up to me and handed me her business card.

"I saw you and thought I should give you this."

"Thanks," I said, looking into her eyes, knowing that despite whatever she was handing me that I had been misjudged and that it was probably not going to help find my phone, stop the crash that took the life of my friend, or affect the way my religious beliefs are now confined to a mere question of shallow tolerance. She smiled back at me, and then left.

Her business card told me that she was a social worker with a foster care agency in Sacramento, which explained her two (presumably) adopted children. She had filled up the back of the card with writing, and it was written:
"www.thework.com," followed by the name Byron Katie who I later looked up and found to be a self-help guru named Byron Kathleen Mitchell who wrote a book titled *Loving What Is*, describing her method of self-inquiry.

"Identify your stressful thought," the woman had written, "then ask the four questions and turn it around." The first of the four questions read: Is it true?

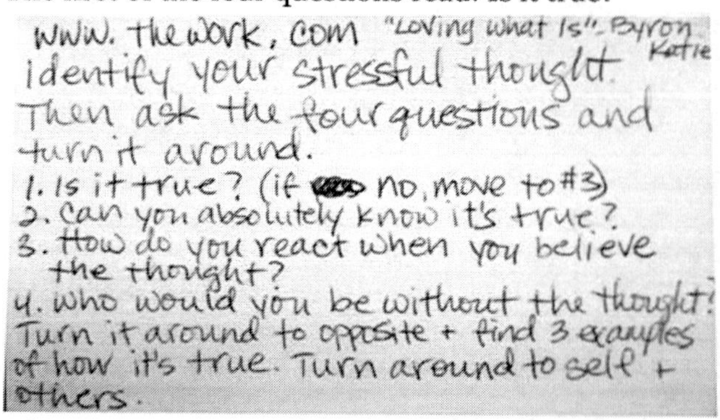
www.thework.com "Loving what is"- Byron Katie
identify your stressful thought.
Then ask the four questions and turn it around.
1. Is it true? (if no, move to #3)
2. Can you absolutely know it's true?
3. How do you react when you believe the thought?
4. Who would you be without the thought?
Turn it around to opposite + find 3 examples of how it's true. Turn around to self + others.

. . . well, I could come up with about a dozen stressful thoughts beginning with illegally hopping a train 450-miles with next to no water and not excused from having another freak accident to imperil things more . . . up to the main reason that I am here: a friend's memorial, not to mention now not having a phone ro get in touch with the people I need to to let know that I am here . . . so yes, I'm afraid it is true . . .

I used a pay phone across the street to call my Mother, the only person besides my current seasonal employer whose number I know off the top of my head. As expected, she was dismayed that I had again managed to lose something of value to me, but was nonetheless relieved to know I was not injured or in jail. Through her I was able to access my phone records online, and by area codes and locales was able to determine which number was my friend Tone's—the only 916 number I had recently called. Thankfully Tone answered his phone, and he picked me up at the south end of the Roseville yard within the hour, T-Box with him, who had, unbeknownst to me, caught-out of the departure tracks the same day in Eugene, just a few hours before I.

In Memory

In Loving Memory Of

JEREMY JOHN GUILL

Date and Place of Birth
February 14, 1980
Sacramento, California

Date and Place of Death
January 4, 2011
Pine Grove, California

January 2011

Sacramento, CA- My presence was for a sober cause, but rarely was I sober. Aside from fruit trees abound with oranges to pick and eat from front yards, Sacramento showed few redeeming qualities. It is a raucous, sprawling, concrete jungle of near-constant debasement, encased by a tangle of race-track-like freeways sped on by frenzied motorists swerving in and out of plumes of exhaust and smoke, always on their way somewhere else in more of a hurry than the other. I found myself surrounded by a solid core of friends who have known each other for years and were now acknowledging the loss of one of their own, and I was more than often in the presence of the immediate family affected by that loss. It was constant turmoil as funeral preparations and Celebration of Life-tributes had to be coordinated on short, tragic notice, on top of the grief of a passing that new details continued to emerge of and color even more heartbreaking. But some of my favorite people in the world were all together in the same place at the same time and we made the best of it. From the house where Wyze was living, to old Taverns, liquor stores, potluck/cookouts, tattoo-shop bonfires, memorials, receptions, and all-night gatherings, it always ended back in the train yard. And that's where we spent the evening before Tone dropped off T-Box and I at the Amtrak station just before midnight. We found a liquor store quick, put the dash in "dine-in" across the street at a Denny's (which left me feeling like *I* had been ripped off since the food was such shit), then scurried into the dark shadows of pillars and bridges behind the Amtrak station to linger until our train arrived.

I have a trail of unused Amtrak tickets that I continue to exchange for new tickets to take me from one station to the next and that I almost always manage to not have torn upon boarding so that I can repeat the process

X

GUILL, Jeremy John

Born February 14, 1980 in Sacramento. Went home to join his mom Judi Ellis on January 4, 2011. Jeremy is survived by his father John Guill, grandson to Leland Guill, and the late Edna Guill. Also survived by grandparents Spencer & Arleen Ellis, sisters Felicia, Jessica & Brooke Guill, brother J.T., numerous aunts, uncles, cousins & nephew Avery, all who loved & adored him, including his best friends Jesse & Darren, his STC "crew", and a host of many, all who Jeremy considered family. Jeremy was a prankster who would put you in stitches with his humor and antics. Jeremy enjoyed drawing, painting but most of all motorcycling in the hills. He is and always will be greatly missed. A memorial will take place on Tuesday, January 11, 2011 at 10:00 AM at **Andrews & Grellich**, 3939 Fruitridge Rd.

over. The latest is a Eugene-to-Salem ticket I purchased back in November and rode all the way to Portland on without having torn. Worth $21, I exchanged it in Sacramento a few days ago and paid an extra $10 to get a new ticket to Chico. T-Box, meanwhile, had an Amtrak voucher he used in exchange for a ticket back north, though I tried to sell him on my scam.

At 0200 it came: the #14 Coast Starlight. I noticed that some people already had seating-assignment slips from checking in their baggage earlier, and the Car Attendant was not checking those people's tickets but only assigning them a seat, yet meanwhile was tearing the tickets of each individual who did not already have a seating-assignment slip. Processing this quickly, I pulled out an old seating-assignment slip I had saved and that had written on it in pencil EUG in three big letters along with seat #50. I placed the old seating-assignment slip on top of the envelope that had my actual ticket in it (a ticket only to Chico), and handed it to the Car Attendant saying, "Eugene," vociferously. She took my word and never looked at the ticket, and even though my seating-assignment slip already had a seat number written on it (which I did foolishly try to hide by folding it over), the Car Attendant took the end of her pencil, erased the old number, and wrote a new seat—#58—that corresponded with her seating-chart. I boarded, went straight to the viewing car, and waited until the train departed Sacramento and the Car Attendant had walked up to her sleeping car before I walked back to an empty seat on a different car and settled in for the night.

A few hours later, whenever the train did arrive in Chico, a different car-attendant came through and told the kid across the aisle from me to get up and get downstairs, that we were in Chico. That Car Attendant then turned to me and asked where I was going (because I did not put the seating-assignment slip above my seat).

"Eugene," I replied. And with that he nodded and walked away.

morning train

I woke at first light to a foggy, dream-like winter landscape passing swiftly by the window of the train. With the Sacramento ambling frigidly around snowy stones to my right. I knew we must be approaching Dunsmuir. Pristine white snow caked the firs and thick fog hovered in between strands and out over the river's course-idyllic in every way and by far the most beautiful I have seen Northern California.

With Castle Crag's craggy crowns obscured by fog, I opened the window on the lower level and leaned my head out as the train glided in sync with the river through Dunsmuir's arctic yard and into town.

winter wonderland

The scenery, though exquisite in beauty, just didn't look as real, nor did I feel as present sitting behind the brown-tinted plexiglas of the Amtrak viewing car. It remained most memorable when I awoke to it in the solitude of my own window seat. But even then, the sounds that make riding trains so tangible, and the smells that accompany the rails—the simmering tracks, coal, oil, grease, and diesel exhaust—were not present to hold my interest for long. The continuation of the trip was no less marvelous, just harder to appreciate amongst a crowd of viewing-car tourists, Christian-meditationist hipsters, giddy pre-teen girls pecking at laptops, an obnoxious redneck talking too loud, a fat ass in Family Guy-pajamas eating potato chips, and Momma's-boys trying slickly to talk up Daddy's-girls for whatever shallow moral boost it was worth—an overall awful noise.

 Minus and Emer in K-Falls

Railroad signals tangle traffic

The three barricades malfunction for at least 90 minutes in downtown Eugene

One car after another approached the railroad crossing at Lawrence Street between West Third and Fourth avenues in downtown Eugene Friday afternoon – and stopped at the lowered crossing arm. And watched the flashing red lights. And listened to the clanging bell warning them a train was approaching. And waited.

But no train was coming. Not for most of the 90 minutes or so, anyway, that three gate crossings on the Union Pacific Railroad tracks were closed.

The closed crossings, at the Lincoln, Lawrence and Washington street crossings, resulted in scores of frustrated motorists deciding to just go ahead and drive their vehicle around the gates and across the tracks from about 3:30 p.m. to 5 p.m.

Some chose to just turn around, including a Lane Transit District EmX bus that had to awkwardly back up at the intersection of Lawrence and West Fourth, bending itself like an accordion.

Tom Weaver, a ShelterCare employee, took matters into his own hands at the Washington Street crossing and turned himself into a cross-

Railroad: 'That's just never a good idea'

A call to Union Pacific, which operates the train tracks, provided little information as to why the gates were stuck.

An employee who answered the phone in "signal operations" in Omaha, Neb., where Union Pacific is based, said he was aware of the problem but was not allowed to say what happened.

"All I know is it's been repaired," said the man who declined to give his name. Asked if there was a local railroad number in Eugene to call for more information, the man said there was but he declined to provide it.

A Union Pacific employee was on the scene during the incident, at one point on his hands and knees looking at a map as he spoke on the phone from inside a control room at the Lincoln Street crossing. The employee said he had no idea what was causing the problem.

Only one train came through, about 4:35 p.m., while the gates were stuck.

Weaver was worried because so many cars had just been crossing a block away at Lawrence Street.

As the train approached, Weaver got a startled look in his eyes.

"Did you see that!" he said. "A lady just rode in front of the train down there on her bike."

Union Pacific to improve local lines

By Ilene Aleshire
The Register-Guard

Union Pacific Railroad is spending about $33.5 million to improve its rail line between Oakridge and Harrisburg and to improve its rail yard in Eugene.

The company is installing 26 miles of new track and more than 81,000 railroad ties as part of a 75-mile track improvement project that is scheduled to be com-

Rail: Union Pacific reporting higher demand from shippers

pleted at the end of March, Hunt said. It also will resurface more than 100 road crossings, which should make for a smoother ride for motorists, he said.

Safety is a big reason for the improvements, Hunt said.

"There is no steering wheel in a locomotive, it's bound to the track," he said. "So you have to make sure the track is in excellent condition."

Improvements to the track, and to the rail yard in Eugene, also mean trains can maintain speed on the track and rail cars can be uncoupled and trains put back together quickly in the rail yard, he said, which is of critical importance to Union Pacific's competitiveness, he said.

The company has a little more than 1,000 miles of track and about 1,600 employees in Oregon, he said.

Railroad crossing closed for repairs

The Union Pacific railroad crossing at Awbrey Lane will be closed from 7 a.m. today until 5 p.m. Thursday while repairs are made to the tracks at the crossing.

Eastbound traffic can travel south on Prairie Road to Irving Road, east on Irving to Northwest Expressway, then north on Prairie Road to Irvington Drive. Westbound traffic can travel south on Northwest Expressway to Irving Road, west on Irving to Prairie Road, then north on Prairie Road to Irvington Drive.

Eugene City, OR

Skinners Butte- Eugene

Welding foreman Richard Kerr, left, of Wisconsin, with Randy Hulse of Idaho, talk about the rail work they just completed.

David Patton/Democrat-Herald

Union Pacific workers load up their machinery Monday after they finished replacing rail near Halsey.

Rail replacement job completed

Crew pulls out for Nevada after installing 24 miles of new track

BY ALEX PAUL
ALBANY DEMOCRAT-HERALD

SHEDD — Union Pacific repairmen are packing up and heading to Nevada today after completing a 24-mile track replacement project between here and Eugene.

"We have been replacing old rail with new, heavy-duty rail," said welding foreman Richard Kerr. "The old stuff was just worn out."

Kerr said the crew is down to about 112 people from an average of about 125, who worked 10- to 12-hour shifts.

The project started in mid-February. Crew members came from throughout the United States and worked eight days on and seven days off. They work in any of the 23 states in which the Union Pacific has track. In Oregon, there are 1,073 miles of it.

Kerr is from Wisconsin. Other workers are from Minnesota, Idaho, Louisiana, Tennessee, Nevada and Arizona.

William Arnold, pictured at the Geary Street railroad crossing near his house on Denver Street S.E., is trying to get the Union Pacific and Portland & Western railroads to cut down on the amount of time engineers blow their horns at Albany crossings.

Train noise irks resident

He says long horn blasts are disrupting his sleep, and he's gathering signatures to take to the Albany council

William Arnold says train engineers blow their horns for far too long at street crossings in his Albany neighborhood, so he is taking steps to try to get something done.

One time during the night, he said a hor sounded for a solid 45 minutes while a train sa near his house.

He said between 25 and 28 Union Pacific freights go through Albany in a 24-hour period, and the Portland & Western operates an other three to seven. Amtrak's Coast Starligh and Cascades passenger trains also pas through the neighborhood.

March 2011

Eugene, OR- It's balmy out. That's what the waitress at Keystone said this afternoon as Sam and I gorged on buckwheat pancakes. It's windy too, and without a drop of rain (it was all spent yesterday), temperatures are at about 60-degrees with the sun occasionally breaking through the clouds—the type of Oregon day when you might spot a rainbow at any given moment.

At dusk, the sun retired slowly behind a heavy sky and I made my way down the Northwest Hwy, eyeing a northbound train on the far tracks having its air hoses checked, and was meanwhile simultaneously being eyed by a worker on the rear of a line of trains backing into the Industry tTacks. I stayed motionlessly visible until it became dark enough, then crossed the Industry Tracks and disappeared into the yard where the northbound train sat hissing. There were several options to ride in case of sudden departure, but nothing preferred (especially in case of rain), and the very last car on the line, an old MP with Freddy, was the only open boxcar, but its doorway exposed, facing west into the lights of the yard office. After walking the line on both sides, I sat atop a car of huge rotund logs and drank all the beer I had just listening to the sounds of the yard. When I later climbed into the MP boxcar I saw its floor coming up at both ends like there had been an earthquake inside and the panels uplifted. I could actually see the ground and wheel axels through the floor on the front end so I laid in the back corner in the shadows. I did not bother putting my earplugs in, and instead focused on the constant multitude of hissing, snapping, popping pistons from nearby idling engines that echoed through the boxcar every split-second. Occasionally a thunderous clanking of steel would reverberate on the track adjacent, jarring the entire boxcar like it were moving. Engines revved up and died down, backed up, picked up, and moved adjacent lines, and a train horn blared somewhere off in the distance. In all its chaos I felt relaxed—this is beauty to me. Though a polluted, rusty, industrial jungle completely opposite a place like Mt. Pisgah, it is beautiful to me in much the same way. Having spent so much time here I've come to cherish the solitude and privacy it affords me, and thinking on that I drifted off to sleep full and content.

rickety old boxcar

Later, the train pulled down to the Departure Tracks from a long slow crawl out of the yard. It proved to be a little hairy getting out of there. The very last car on the line screeched and rattled raucously back and forth as a white jeep followed the train, paralleling my boxcar the entire way. A worker switched the tracks and the train rolled slowly toward a pair of headlights shining brightly in through the boxcar door. As the train creaked along slower and slower I felt increasingly worried that the last car would stop right in front of that jeep and someone would look inside and pull me off. But oh-so-slowly my boxcar crept by. The train stopped briefly beside a large lumberyard just north of Eugene, then finally pulled onto the mainline and began to highball. Bumping and bouncing along the dark land, through Junction City, across the Willamette River, along sowed fields spanning to the dark, milky horizon, the train felt like it might splinter and fall apart at any second—by far the bumpiest ride I have been on in a long time, which reminded me of my first ever train ride: a Disko grainer to Kansas City some years ago, balled up in the rear cubbyhole at the back end of a long junk train being thrust violently back and forth as the train clanked, shunted, and jerked endlessly along the miserable Missouri landscape. I remember thinking then that if I ever rode a train again I would surely have to wear a bicycle-helmet the next time. Now, trying to lie down in the back corner was preposterous thinking that I could get any sleep. On a surprisingly warm night, I stood leaning out the doorway with the wind at my face, watching the valley roll by jas I have so many times before. And as the train continued to rock violently, I had to be extra careful to not end up another Michael Andrew Birkinshaw (the train had slacked and shunted with such a force already that it nearly jolted me out the boxcar door)!

Stopping at Shedd alongside a rancid smelling cattle pasture and a cesspool pond of some sort with a road on the other side of that, a red light shone ahead . . . *With all Amtraks through for the night it could only be another freight this train is waiting on. (As long as I'm not at Marion I'm really not concerned.) It smells pretty fucking rancid as I stand pissing on the mainline watching Freddy's blink reflecting off the tracks toward two distant signal lights. It's warm out still, probably about sixty, and that and the wind doesn't help the stench any* . . . The signal south turned green and minutes later headlights appeared distantly ahead as a southbound approached. It roared past in a whirlwind of lights with two DPUs, and after it cattle stench filled the boxcar and frogs croaked wildly in the trackside watershed. The train stopped abruptly again before Albany, on the mainline behind the corrugated-metal Oregon RV Appliance Repair shed, where again, frogs croaked incessantly in the confusion, perhaps wondering if each other frog was OK. (I've heard this before in a train yard in Watsonville California, where the mainline borders acres of Driscoll strawberry fields and where every time a train passed on the mainline and I stepped out of the yard into the furrows I would hear frogs down in the watershed at the base of the ballast croaking wildly about all the confusion) . . . *No doubt it must be putrid, as these amphibians are, cruelly, living in chemical runoff from the tracks. It's sad, but precious at the same time as they communicate to maintain some Anuran solidarity . . .*

Shedd at night

I woke in the morning on a siding somewhere north of Salem . . . *Marion County probably* . . . where acres of grass(seed) sprawled out from the boxcar door and heavy clouds lingered west above distant I-5. Swollen fields held large puddles and a small single-engine plane flew back and forth over the land very low. It almost seemed like a remote control gig but was most likely spraying the fields. A very short train then blew by—the 0530 Cascades from Eugene making its morning run north. My train pulled forward a little bit, but only to stop again and I had no idea what was happening so I fell back asleep. Several hours later

wide open Willamette Valley

the train was on the move again, passing through Woodburn, where a small cemetery on the north side of town marks the spot from which southbound trains often stop on the mainline to work. I realized then that I had been sided at Gervais—north of Salem indeed. Shortly thereafter, the train violently cut its air, stopping abruptly on the mainline again, the smell of burnt rubber snuffing my nose. I wondered if the train had possibly hit something or was just malfunctioning badly. It sat on the mainline in a hilly area around a bend where a little road wraps through the hills (a dirt access road or perhaps someone's driveway). A worker walked back and I heard him fooling around the back of the boxcar I was in, but he didn't look inside. The train then slowly pulled up to unblock a road crossing and I suspected the worker was riding the ladder on the back of the car so I remained still. But I don't know what happened to him . . . *It has been a manically unstable ride all the way from those rickety departure tracks in Eugene and I am quickly losing faith in my train. I feel like it's just going to splinter and fall apart or leave me here altogether . . .*

A malfunction of some sort definitely destabilized the train because after rolling again it again blew its air abruptly as smoke rose from the brake pads several car-lengths ahead and the train stopped dead on the mainline before reaching Coalca. I walked around the wooded riverbank there and was just about to climb back into the boxcar when I checked back at the last second to make sure no one was looking and but sure enough saw a worker in a bright green vest walking back my side of the train. I pretended to be taking pictures in case he saw me, then walked around the back of the train with a wide berth and, watching his feet from underneath the car, dodged him. He walked to the back end of the train and around it, and as he crossed over I cut through a coupler ahead of him and hopped back over to the other side. Then, as he continued up the other side of the train, I walked back to my boxcar and climbed back inside.

Hwy 99-side, before Coalca

*

Oregon City, OR- What a blower that train was. I rode the last car on the line, a dilapidated old MP boxcar with missing floorboards, and I abandoned it twelve hours later at Coalca after a series of malfunctions. I put my thumb out on Hwy 99 but no one picked me up, and twenty minutes later the malfunctioning train clanked together and rattled off and I said Fuck it! and walked the tracks north.

The section of tracks from Coalca to the recently shuttered Blue Heron Paper Mill in Oregon City follows the Willamette on a high riverbank of enormous, sometimes moss-covered boulders and a vertical cliffside that feeds the river waterfalls of runoff from the roller coaster-like highway it holds. While several dilapidated marina buildings and other undetermined structural remains designate the area largely abandoned, it is rather superb if you take the time to observe its intrinsic qualities. A quaint little neighborhood sits a mile south of Oregon City with houses that face the tracks in an old-timey way and have little white picket fences with waist-high gates opening to pathways crossing the tracks to recreational river access. It looks like a small town on some discontinued shortline in the south and is totally idyllic in that sense . . . *The thought of this being the very same view of the Willamette River the first settlers in Oregon saw two-hundred years ago, and that the Kalapuya Indians had known long before that, is refreshing to my mind. However, behind me the highway cuts brutally through the rest of the landscape and everything is centered around easy access to that concrete trail. And of course Union Pacific renders the riverbank a constant threat, as is apparent from the tracks being strewn with deer carnage and the scattered remains of mammalian skeletons . . .*

It aint fresh!
FLOOR HT 3-8
To BOXHOUND
KCS758152
HERMAN
THE GOLDEN WEST
MFG
OAKLAND
2006
WHAT'S IT ABOUT?
ABOUT 30 SEC. OF MY LIFE.
UNLATCH
TO CLOSE
DOOR
TICKING Time Bomb...!
204500
81500
TTX IS FOR LOSERS!
808
2 INCH HF COMP SHOES
RIP CLOUD.
SP
BOOKMAN! 07
2 INCH HF COMP SHOES
Etaja
11/07/09
FEB.
WARY
1
4

I reached Oregon City with frustrated sweat upon my brow and wandered into a coffee shop to clean up and caffeinate myself for the day. From outside there I caught the #33 bus to Portland. A rather cramped ride to begin with, I had to sit in the front Reserved-For-Handicapped-Persons seats across from a plump, sorry-looking goth girl clutching a library copy of a thick Stephen King novel and who sobbed into her cell-phone to a no doubt equally pathetic boyfriend about her own personal problems as if it were a sorrowing, real-life soap opera. After hanging up she begged for stranger-comfort by making eyes at others and sobbing loudly for all to hear. Her voluminous cleavage and cut-too-short denim skirt was an affront to all taste and decency. And then, if her life couldn't get any worse, the bus broke down at Silver Springs Road with Portland looming visibly on the horizon. The bus just quit, and all passengers—wheelchairs, travel packs (mine), and bikes alike—had to walk down the busy street to the next bus stop and wait to cram into an even-more-crowded next bus . . . *First it was the train that broke down repeatedly, huffing and puffing for hours before even nearing Portland, and now the bus. After getting this far it has taken me three hours just to get another five-miles and I'm not even to Portland yet. I should've went back to sleep and stayed with the train . . .*

broke-down-bus riders

April 2011

Portland, OR- It's not unlike Portland to suddenly revert to winter in the spring with freezing storms that make you run for shelter. While walking through the shadows of the already-wet train cars in Albina yard, a rogue sleet began and continued relentlessly, thick and visible in the spectrum of the yard's lights. Skittle-sized pellets of ice pummeled down on the Northeast Portland riverbank, careening loudly off the vertical steel walls of boxcars and echoing oddly off empty tankers and hoppers. Wooden crossties became white and slippery to the boot's touch, like from a fresh frost. I took refuge under Going Street, but the bridge is not exactly conducive to human settlement- the concrete slanting up to the road is too steep to climb and there is no room to lie at the top, and the pillars below comprise one of Portland's HIViest areas, to say the least. One headless line of trains sat on the Departure Tracks extending north past the bridge and after the sleet had quelled to a drizzle I called several of the cars in to find them destined for midwestern towns days and nights away. Because the stock was mostly bound for BNSF yards (one of them interchanging at a BNSF location in Washington and several others going to Minnesota), my feeling was that the train was headed north, mostly likely to Seattle to interchange, then heading east. On an ALY boxcar with no seal, I opened the door, put my stuff inside, and with some beer I picked up at my favorite convenient store (the Plaid Pantry at the top of the hill on Interstate Ave.), I sat in the boxcar door staring out into the wet night.

Around 2200 a northbound train pulled down the mainline and stopped—a line of mostly empty well-cars. It was Seattlebound, I presumed, and though wet, suicidal, and exposed to perhaps even more wet, I climbed aboard and found somewhat of a ledge to lay on at the front end of one of the cars so that if the rain did again come, it would do so at an angle and spare me as much as possible.

*

I woke up somewhere in Washington getting dumped on—sound asleep, just getting dumped on. The train was sided and I could soon feel the wet beginning to seep through to my clothes as it collected in the grooves of my sleeping mat. I got my umbrella out and packed up my sopping sleeping bag and just sat there in the rain. (There's something about the alignment our solar body in the spring and the relative declination of the Pacific Northwest that just seems to suck the moisture from the sky at sunrise and sunset, the same way that the clouds then burn off around noon and reveal the day, only to reappear again around dusk.) With the sun rising bright in the overcast east and the landscape agriculturally nondescript—a barb-wired-in distribution warehouse, I-5 moving along two-hundred

somewhere in Washington

yards to the west under lush, glistening hills with fog cutting through the evergreens—I felt like I was still in the Wapato Valley. Looking ahead down the tracks my train looked to be snaking out from the siding onto the mainline blocking it, but that was not the case. A series of long, drawn out horns eventually led to a southbound hotshot, and before it passed entirely, the empty train I sat on clanked together and rolled off along the wet Washington landscape. Catching up to the rain that had previously woken and soaked me, I put my umbrella up and sat helplessly under it with my back to the front of the well-car, hunched up with my knees in my sweatshirt trying to warm my painfully cold hands. Urbanity reigned on both sides of the tracks confining me to remain down so that the only things I could see were the ground passing below and occasionally the tops of trains as I passed them . . . *I don't know where I am but my best guess is nearing Tacoma . . .*

On several occasions I tried to take notice of my surroundings, hoping to gauge some sort of claim on my trajectory, but nothing proved useful. (I saw Emerald Downs, a racetrack or something that I thought looked familiar, a sign designating the Black River, a small wooden trestle following it, and a multitude of BNSF freightage and rail equipment.) Suddenly the valley seemed to dissolve and immense hills grew around the train. Arms of the freeway overlapped in myriad spans, wrapping around each other and ultimately transporting the entire I-5 corridor to the east side of the tracks. More idle trains were passed and a Puget Sound Sounder snuck up from behind, no doubt seeing me plain as day sitting down in the well—that's when I knew I must be close. Busier and busier the landscape became as what looked like an airport took to the west side of the train and multiple tracks fed an increasing intermodel presence suggesting a nearby port: the Puget Sound. But I could not see water. The train then passed under a large scaffolding archway with the name Georgetown on it, telling, no doubt, but I didn't even have my maps to figure out where that was. As the train slowed its roll I almost hopped off in case the Sounder had called me in, but when it continued on I stayed with it. I could tell by looking at the ground below that the train had switched tracks and veered off the mainline, but again I had not done my research like I should have and when I looked up and

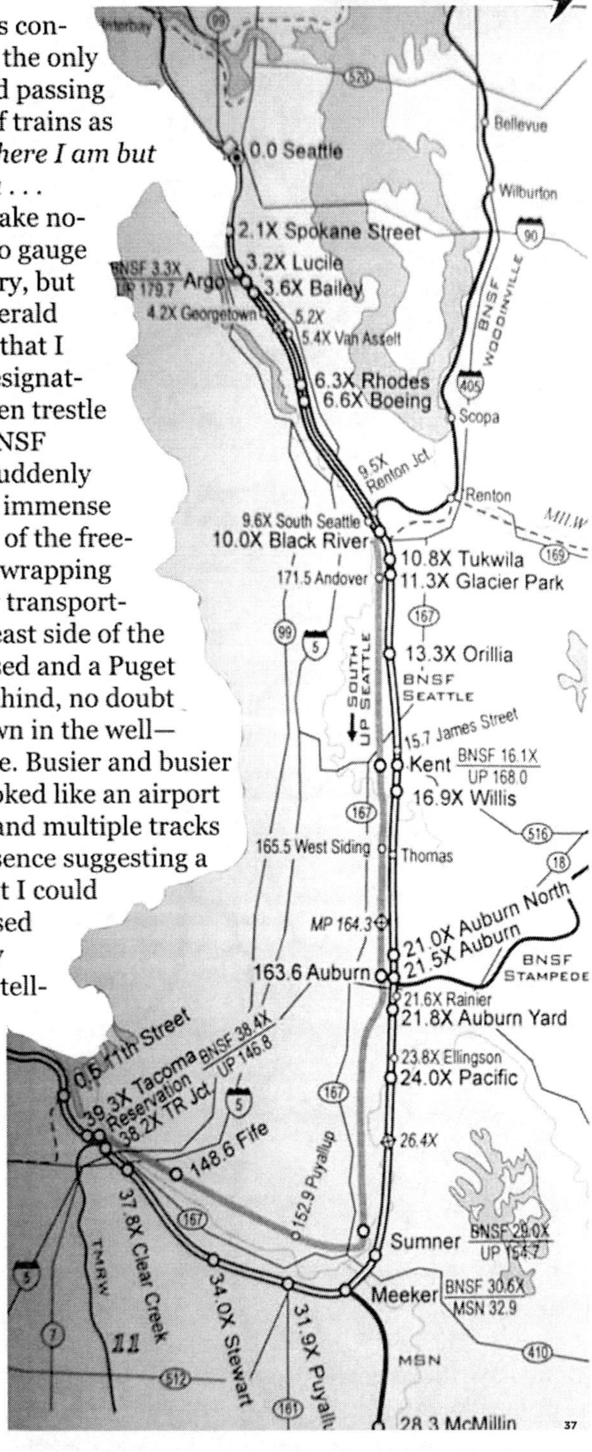

saw an inter-model yard with the name Argo, it only sounded vaguely familiar. Two workers stood on both sides of the train ahead operating a remote control engine and my train car stopped beside one them. Vulnerable anyhow, I stood up knowing the worker would see me but hoping he would not care, or at least that I could get safely out of the yard before anything could happen.

Argo entrance

"Whoooooa!" he exclaimed, obviously taken aback. He looked at his partner to confirm what he was seeing as I hopped off the train and walked up to him.

"You know that's illegal?" he asked in an obvious rhetorical question.

"Yessir!" I responded. "Can you tell me where is Argo?"

"Your in Seattle," he said, pointing to a distant dreary cityscape on the horizon that I then turned to see for myself.

"Yes! I made it."

"Where are you trying to go?"

"Seattle."

"Where did you get on?"

"Portland. Last night."

"Really?"

"Thank you sir," I said, ending our brief conversation, "I'm getting out of the yard." And with that I walked briskly out of the yard and to a nearby street where I stood to catch the #106 bus to downtown.

Seattle, WA- Seattle is wet and gray and cold and not unlike I imagined it would be: spitting rain. I am hanging out with Read, a graffiti artist wanted in several states, apparently (according to *The Stranger*), and he is putting the final touches on his first gallery show as part of the Lawrimore Project, on dis-

BLART

What it is: A page from *The Reader*
Where it is: Inside a 2005 book by Read (www.operationmadman.com)

Read—usually seen in block letters—is the signature of a graffiti artist wanted in several states. His hardcover little black book, *The Reader*, is a cult hit and "a mix tape of the last 100 years of graphic design." The description comes from artist Elias Hansen, a longtime friend of Read's who's now curating Read's first-ever gallery show (at Lawrimore Project, opening Thursday during art walk). The show will be collages, screen prints, and pieces painted directly on the walls (maybe some will appear on Seattle streets?)—the artist won't be at the opening, naturally. "Perhaps jail lies

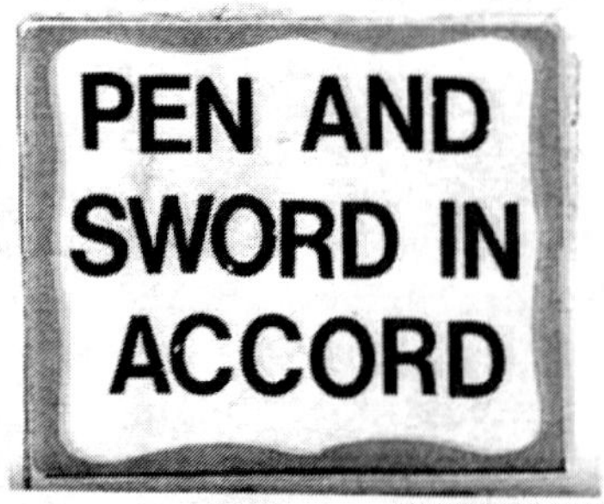

COURTESY OF THE ARTIST

ahead," Hansen wrote in his catalog essay introducing Read. "Maybe he'll get beat up. He could go crazy. I've definitely seen that happen. Some guys get nerve damage. They start pissing themselves in the night... It would be hard not to explain Read as a gamer, an operator, an *agent* in the truly intentional sense. But this isn't liberation and salvation. We're in the thick of it. If there were a way to explain it, I would have already." **JEN GRAVES**

play inside a small storefront in a renovated, old architectural office building in Pioneer Square, a skuzzier part of downtown. He has been up all night for the second night in a row hanging pieces, finishing an enormous black roller that looks like it could only have been accomplished with the aide of a projector, but wasn't, and organizing several hijacked newspaper boxes that he has repainted and claimed to display his own book *The Reader*—all inside this little bathroom-sized space with a high ceiling.

It was my first time in Seattle and Read and Herman Beans cordially showed me around. We spent the hours before the opening drinking at The Central, Seattle's oldest saloon (established in 1896), where a buffet of cheese ravioli and mini-hot dogs adorned the corner. The dark, musty interior of The Central made me feel right at home as I drank Manny's, a local beer that everyone seems to prefer by the pitcher. By eveningtime hotdog vendors and shoe-shiners had set up on the sidewalk outside and patrons began to pour in from Friday's Art Walk. The night was a wild success (critics agree!), and one to remember on the streets of Seattle. Long after the gallery had closed, some envious person threw a stereo-speaker through the front window, breaking the glass and gouging the plaster on the back wall but otherwise doing no damage to anything. And no one really cared either. I think it enhanced the show, and if anything added to Read's credibility as a street artist. Last-call later, five shots rang deafeningly into the misty night air, echoing across the Sound and through the brick alleyways of Pioneer Square, people scattering in all different directions.

Read at the Lawrimore Project in Seattle

([background noise]

ME: ...buckin' shots.

READ: You guys all got fuckin' hella shook!

ME: That was the loudest thing I've heard in months man!

[Read laughs]

READ: Was that shit pretty loud?

ME: It was so loud! It was echoing all across the bay... echoing all across the Sound.

[background noise]

READ: Fuck. Isn't it crazy someone just... threw that fuckin' shit through the window?

ME: Ya. While you were buckin' shots, right? Coincidence? Who knows...

DRUNKEN BROAD: Definitely obnoxious coincidence.

[Read looking for his phone charger]

READ: Is this my charger?

ME: you're not gonna find that thing in this mess.

READ: Alright. Fuck it... find that shit tomorrow.

[van door shuts]

DRUNKEN BROAD: What are you doing? Don't you know what you're doing?

[inaudible talking]

DRUNKEN BROAD to ME: You get it, right?

READ: Let's Go! Call Jamie. See if Jamie still wants to hang out.

ME to DRUNKEN BROAD: Halfway...

DRUNKEN BROAD: What the fuck are you doing with a gun you have to shoot into a bush at the same time this weird random coincidence at the same time happens that you don't know anything about?

ME: What hath Fortuna spun my way?

READ: I didn't shoot that shit in the bush. I shot it in the air...)

Tacoma mainline from caboose

April 2011

Tacoma, WA- I preyed on trains from the Amtrak station, which conveniently borders a small BNSF yard just down the street from the Greyhound station on Puyallup Ave., where there are also two gas stations to acquire food and beer while waiting. The tracks here are fairly busy considering both UP and BNSF share trackage rights, as well as Amtrak which runs at least six trains a day. Just south of the Amtrak station is a loading dock that had several boxcars backed up to it, across from which the yard sat fairly full. However, no trains were on the outer five mainlines, which meant that everything was either being received or classified which was about the way it looked to me as there were no units in sight. It being Saturday and the business with the loading dock closed, I sat there writing and watching. Directly across from me sat an old green BN caboose made into the middle of a string of miscellaneous cars that I had my eye on from minute-one. After several patient moments of looking out, I crossed the tracks to find the caboose wide open and accepting of me. Actually, it presented the perfect place to wait. It had a bed, desk, table and chairs, two second-level seats that looked out over the top the trains, and several compartments to hide stuff in. I could've stayed there for days!

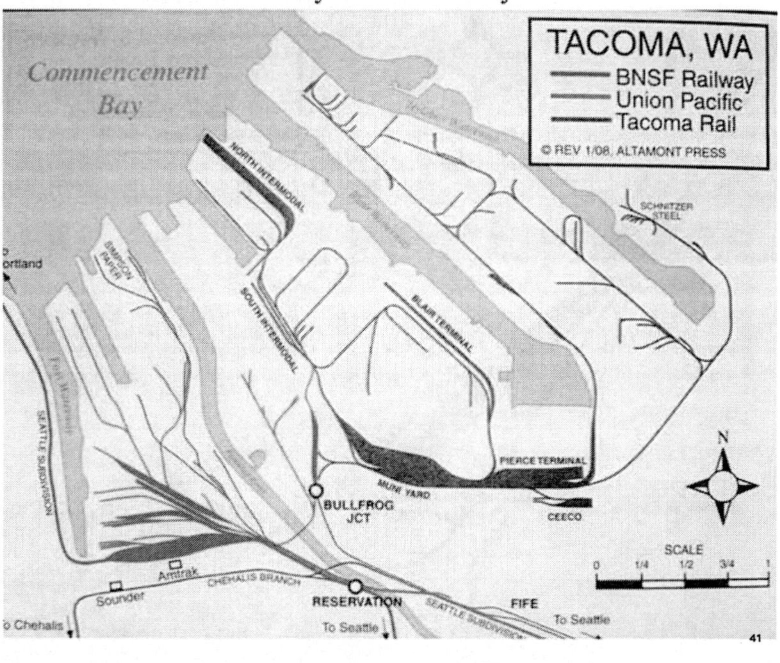

The mainline quickly proved to be extremely active, as thought, with three northbounds (two BNSF and one UP) moving through, one of which stopped for about an hour to work. I made a beer run across the street and found an obscure beer called *Schmidt*, with one of the most

Pocatello Paul
PLATE
HOBO YORS
DERASER
TG
NOBODY CAN SEE US
THE GENTRY
Ewok
M.B.D 1-29-10
FU MAN
Foot Long Frank Mrugala
JUNE 09
RMS ACQUITANIA
2008.
U.S.A. Japan GERMANY

Tacoma, WA

atrocious labels I have ever seen—a sepia-toned buck standing in the woods as if it were being viewed through the scope of a rifle. That's what I purchased a six-pack of and drank while sitting in the upper-level of the caboose looking out across the yard. It soon became apparent that, at least on this day, southbounds are not as frequent as northbounds. Trains destined for Seattle, Everett-and-beyond, and British Columbia-bound coal cars almost never stopped coming through, and most of them I could have caught on the fly (I think), if I needed to. I actually contemplated catching-out north and reestablishing myself back up in Seattle for a clean catch south, out of Argo. But then again, I really didn't have any idea how these southbounds behaved and I didn't want to give up on Tacoma so soon. Besides, I was pretty comfortable in the caboose.

It was a nice day in Tacoma, which doesn't necessarily mean warm or sunny—just not raining. Derived from the native "Tahoma," a name given to the great mountain looming over the city, Tacoma sits south of the yard on a jut of land in the Commencement Bay part of Puget Sound. A railroad town founded in the late 1800s by Northern Pacific Railway, Tacoma very much has the feeling of a port city with an array of bridges linking to nearby islands. There are docks galore, seafood restaurants, a waterfront conducive to people-traffic that stretches the length of the city's shoreline, and boats—in harbors, at ports, docking and undocking—surrounding the city at bay. Tacoma is not a sprawling expanse, but rather a town stacked on steep hills that provide an upper-handed view across the Sound, of Vashon Island (the second longest [behind Long] island in the continental U.S., which stretches all the way to Seattle), and of monumental, glaciated, fine beer-inspiring Mt. Rainier dominating the eastern horizon. Unfortunately, I did not get to spend much time in Tacoma, but perhaps another day...

*

BILL VIRGIN

At its heart, this is still a rail town

Today's events marking the centennial of Tacoma's Union Station are really two commemorations in one. May 1 also marks the 40th anniversary of Amtrak's launch.

But then, May is a momentous month for rail history as it relates to Tacoma; May 10 will be the 142nd anniversary of the driving of the Golden Spike in Utah to complete the country's first transcontinental rail link. That touched off a flurry of ventures to build other routes to the West Coast, which led to the Northern Pacific's efforts to get to Puget Sound, which led to Tacoma's brief status as the winner of the Northwest's terminus sweepstakes, and you know the story since then.

Tacoma is also one of the few towns in the U.S. with its own railroad, that being the municipally owned Tacoma Rail which operates over 204 miles of track. Tacoma Rail has been heavily reliant on container traffic into and out of the port, which hasn't been a robust business. In recent years it's been looking at what it might do with its lines outside the Tideflats beyond providing storage space for idled container cars (which it has done). In recent weeks it has announced new customers including a scrap-steel sorting facility at

Frederickson that will use Tacoma Rail to move containers between the industrial park and the seaport.

The current and future relevance of rail to Tacoma is evident in ongoing debates about moving Amtrak trains to the Point Defiance cutoff through Lakewood – thus relieving some freight congestion – and proposals for enlarging the Stampede Pass tunnel to accommodate double-stack container cars and provide more east-west freight capacity.

While discussions still rage about the viability of passenger rail, especially in the long-haul market, there are few such questions about the freight side of the business. There are some commodities and products that are just too big and too heavy to move economically on land except by rail. The big money seems to think so. Warren Buffett famously made his "all-in bet on the American economy" by buying the part of BNSF he didn't already own. The largest individual shareholder in Canadian National? Bill Gates.

Saturday May 7 is National Train Day, with events scheduled at Lacey, Kelso, Bellingham and Snoqualmie. In Tacoma, it's been Train Day every day for most of its history – and likely will be in its history still to come.

Bill Virgin is editor and publisher of Washington Manufacturing Alert and Pacific Northwest Rail News.

By evening's onset seven northbound trains had come through, four of which were catchable on the fly. The seventh northbound was a damn-fast line of BNSF maroon hoppers and after that the first southbound pulled into the yard, a short line of doublestacks that did not seem too promising, so I made another six-pack-of-Schmidt run.

The 8th northbound of the day, a loaded BNSF coal train doing a good 35 - 40 mph, was no doubt headed to Vancouver, B.C. for export. I saw very, very few markings on that line of silver-bullets, but it had two DPUs pushing. The ninth northbound was another line of BNSF maroons . . . *Whistle Blower, 7/09- Low Expectations; Joins; DCH Bend Over Oregon; Texican Gothic; and several Ewoks* . . . A DPU pushed this line as well, which suggested it too is going a longer distance than just Seattle.

I finally lost track of how many northbounds came through—ten or eleven or twelve—but another southbound did finally pull into the yard after sunset, and not a stock of cars that I had seen occupying the yard thus far, which made me think it was not going to stay. After cutting its air, the unit's broke off carrying with them the first half of the train. In the cover of darkness I left the caboose and walked the line back. It consisted of a lot of Canadian grainers, old BN hoppers, and obscure boxcars that I quickly determined were loaded. After walking both sides of the line I found the only rideable to be a big-belly Canadian hopper with a filthy porch facing into the wind. But since it's spring in the rainy Northwe(s)t, I needed to find something more suitable to ride. Most of the boxcars had seals on their doors so I didn't try to open them, but I then came upon an NOKL boxcar without a seal and managed to open its door, and it was indeed empty (however there was still a seal on the other-side's door). I placed my bags inside the boxcar and rested my feet by dangling my legs out the door. A unit passed behind me on the mainline and I climbed over and saw it to be southbound too, but I didn't get to see if the units were UP or BNSF. The train was short too, anyhow, and though it stopped briefly, I let it go and went back to the boxcar.

Trains clanked on the shove, my boxcar lurched, and the train eventually departed south on a steady curve about the dark shimmering bay, passing under cathedral-like bridges, through multiple industries, past grain mills and sidings

departing Tacoma

stocked with a plethora of BNSF maroon hoppers stretching for miles, cut through a short tunnel beneath an overpass and then delved into a longer tunnel that stretched for about a mile—the Nelson-Bennet Tunnel. Curving eastward underneath Point Defiance and submerging me in as great a pitch-black as I have known, the tunnel then spit the train out along the eastern shore of the Puget Sound . . . *The tunnel was a good mile long and I could not see my hand passing over my face . . . just pitch-black for a good two or three minutes and the train came out right along the Sound . . . now just barreling along its shore . . . It's wide open and there's an arch-bridge ahead, a big Golden Gate-like bridge arching over the Sound . . . There's an island in the middle and the Sound looks like the Willamette up in Oregon City if the Willamette were three or four times as wide, wider than the Columbia . . . It's beautiful and wide and dark and milky and now reminds me of the Gorge as the train rounds along banks of huge boulders, occasionally passing slender sand beaches . . . I can see why the early explorers once mistook this for the mouth of the Northwest Passage . . . barreling along . . . A train approaches in the distance with bright headlights . . . now diverging readily from the Sound and going over a sort of dried-up area where the water has receded like at low tide . . . Crossing I-5 into a woodsy area . . . still barreling along at 45 - 50 miles per hour, toward Olympia, I suppose . . . The only problem with this boxcar is the door keeps... Every time the train shunts the boxcar's door closes a little bit more and I have to push it back open . . . I know that it's a pressure-release door that won't just lock me inside . . . I mean, I don't think I'm going to get stuck in here, but I don't want to take any chances . . . I wedged my water bottle, which fit pretty generously, into the crease, and also a beer can, but I don't think that's really going to do any good. Hopefully I won't be locked in this boxcar by morning. If I am, it will be a slow painful death in which dehydration will be the key factor because I have only one bottle of water . . . If I die, I'll die doing what I love . . . a noble cause . . .*

*

I'm somewhere in Washington—not sure where. I slept all night in that boxcar on a siding somewhere, and it rained the whole night, but I was comfortable . . . Now in a yard somewhere in Washington and the train just started moving again . . . wet and gray . . . old BN cars and lumber . . . headed south without any signs telling me where I am (I'll have to figure that out by deduction) . . . moving steady . . . A small lake of some sort to the west of the train car . . . hills across from that with fog clinging to the tops of them . . . very low

southbound in the morning

cloud cover . . . lots of empty and abandoned docks, and posts sticking out of the water . . . Moving steadily at 30- 35 -40 miles per hour through a kind of marshland . . . Everything is wet and gray yet still pretty—milepost 1048—and there's lots of lumber and industry around . . . The lake widens and shows its true character as a bay or marina with boats out—not as wide as the Sound, but still a wide bay . . . this could be Longview, or around there . . . A whole line of trains that were in Tacoma last night are now down here in Washington—Ridgefield . . . They must've passed me in the night, and now I'm passing them . . . Fidel siding . . . Now pulling into Fruit Valley, wherever the fuck that is . . . A lot of familiar cars hanging out in this yard though, that *I can already tell. There's a light, spitting rain and I'm on a jeep path in between two lines. The line I just got off, it's probably going to stay here for a while. However, a line across from it is getting air hose-checked by a guy on an ATV, and taking that to be the line that's going to move first . . . I'm climbing over to it . . . Rain picking up, almost becoming sleet . . . A train horn in the distance sounds like a crossing horn, not a startup horn . . . I hear the train ticking air and even sense it nudge a little bit . . . Workers on ATVs always unnerve me and there looks to be one coming down on each side of the train . . . I've got to get off this porch when the worker comes because I don't know if the cubbyhole's going to cut it . . . Shit!* [sound of ATV revving], *Dude's right across from me on an ATV . . . He just rolled straight past as I hid behind a wheel axel . . . A light rain in Vancouver—I'm just going to go ahead and say this is Vancouver. I've been here for about an hour and no trains have left. That same line of boxcars from last night in Tacoma that passed me and that I then passed at Ridgefield this morning has pulled into the yard and is now sitting on the line next to me. I'm waiting for a move, anything to get me closer to downtown Vancouver so I can just take a bus to Portland . . . There's something coming in between these two trains . . . BNSF coal-cars, loaded, just went north, and there's definitely a guy on an ATV down there working on this line . . . Sounds like an Amtrak coming*

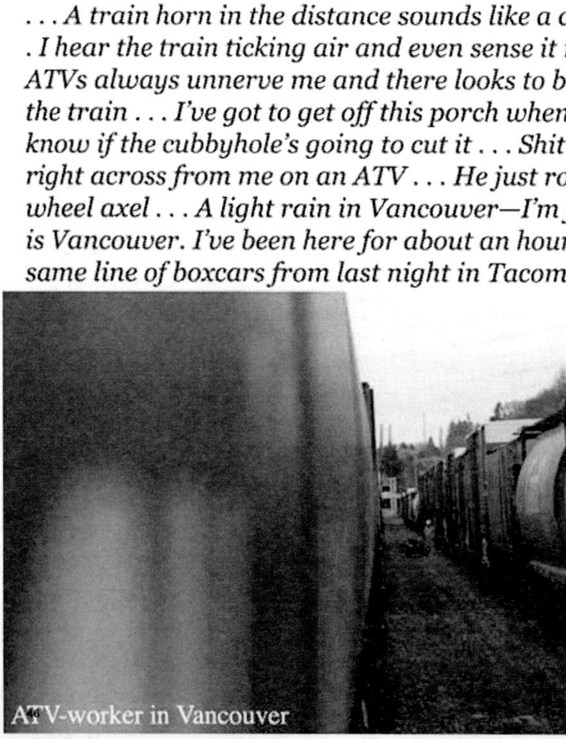

ATV-worker in Vancouver

through . . . [Amtrak approaches] *. . . It's the Cascades . . .* [Amtrak roars by] *. . . Kind of seems like strange timing . . . A guy is coming down my line on an ATV doing something or another—I have to keep an eye on him . . . Just left the north end of that Vancouver yard, or Fruit Valley, or whatever it's called, by jumping on a line when it started to move, then getting off when that line stalled and another line started to move and catching onto that other line on the fly . . . It's spitting rain and I'm on the move again, trying to just get back across the river to Portland. Time will tell where this train will take me, but hopefully it's not headed east. I didn't really think about that. Hopefully I'll be able to get off before then if it is . . . Lots of whistles . . .*

Portland, OR 1200- I was definitely in the Couv. I was there for about two hours and just wanted to get the hell out. It's the worst when you're on the fringe of getting back to town after a trip but just can't quite get all the way there. You can go from Tacoma to Vancouver overnight easily, and then it can take an entire day just to get across the river a few more miles to Portland. I wanted to avoid that and I hopped on the first train that started moving, and when that train stopped and another started to move, I caught onto the other one and rode that one down through the

@ Amtrak

yard. I saw a big Depths piece on a wall and was like yep, that's the Couv. But the train headed east; it ended up veering east, so when it was still going slow and kind of curving between two building-backs, I caught-off. But I did so pretty sloppily, missing the bottom rung, and I took a spill, scraping up my knee (my bad knee of course) but it wasn't too bad. I caught-off pretty much right by the Amtrak station so I walked over to the station, washed up and exchanged an old, unused ticket for a ticket to Salem—a $27 transaction. Outside, a UP train sat idling—a line of Canadian grain-cars with just two units. I could only think that it would go to Albina since it was UP and all, and so I went around to the other side of the tracks by walking under the bridge, waited, caught that train on the fly and rode it across the Columbia River to Peninsula Junction, which runs along a golf course where people were playing (which felt kind of strange because they all could've easily seen me), and when *that* train surprised me by veering east, I caught-off it on the fly just about in front of Peninsula Tunnel that leads to Albina yard. I walked to the tunnel, hiked up over it, and caught the #4 bus at Trenton and Alaska to the MAX stop at Interstate and Lombard, where I transferred to the

rolling through Vancouver yard

crossing the Columbia River

Yellow Line and rode to the Rose Quarter to wait for a train under Steel Bridge . . . *Rolling through Harrisburg in a DPU on the final stretch of the Brooklyn sub . . . Southern Pacific caboose on display . . . 30-miles an hour . . . One more siding before Irving and I'll be back in Eugene. The sun is low in the sky and it's getting dark . . . Lots of cattle and muddy backyards . . . The P&W tracks come into view . . . Picking up momentum bordering the P&W tracks across a junk-laden middle-ground swollen with water and a lot of nothingness . . . Coming up on a slight curve ahead along farmland . . . Super-dark in the east-milky-like— and the earth a very vibrant green . . . Here comes the Farmland and that flooded pasture . . . Looks like grass seed . . . and, rounding the curve, the whole train comes into view and I*

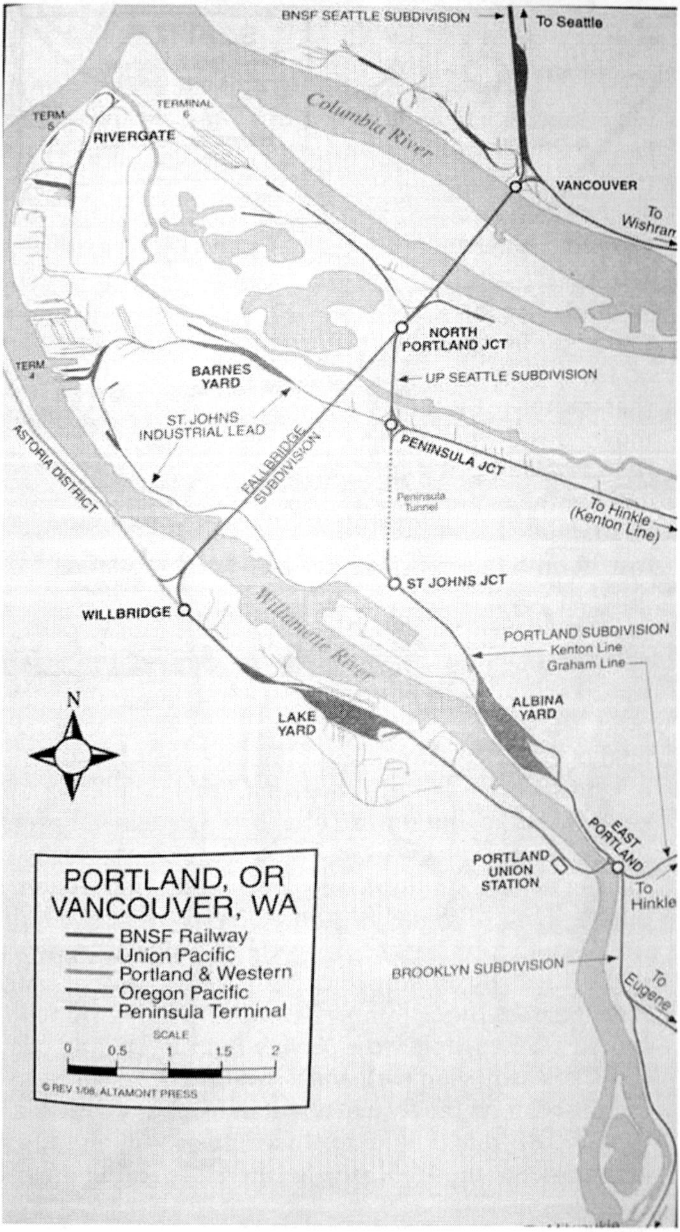

Willamette Valley: from the back of the DPU

can see the tanker cars ahead . . . Telephone poles curve with the line . . . acreage . . . P&W's tracks west . . . The train goes right onto a bridge and crosses the Willamette—the train is rolling onto the bridge. P&W has it's own bridge that looks more like a drawbridge . . . I don't know what the purpose of that is . . . The river high, swollen, swift beneath, rolling, full . . . A secondary-watershed across from that . . . the tracks on a hill of steep ballast, while P&W's tracks are on an old wooden trestle that looks very outdated . . . Now both tracks on steep ballast slopes, and down in between is just a mess of blackberries and swamp and trees and bad bramble and ivy and who-the-fuck-knows . . . Looking back at the bridge and the straightaway behind . . . the train picking up a little bit of momentum as it closes in on the P&W tracks—about maybe twenty yards between them at this point . . . Now Junction City . . . (my favorite leg of this trip is between Harrisburg and Junction City and it's very short—maybe only four, five, six, seven miles) . . . Do your chain hang low?

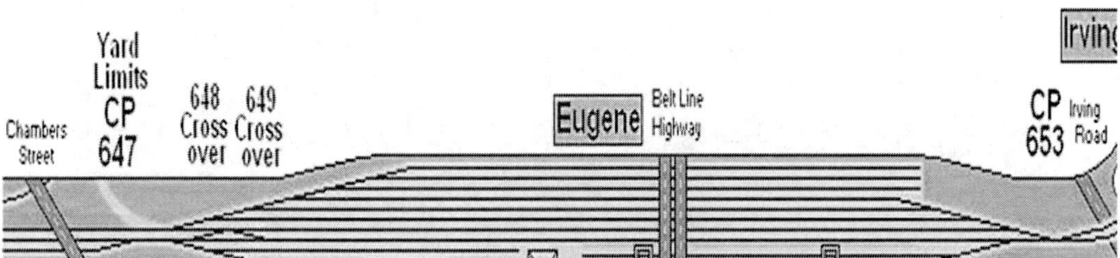

R.I.P. Jesse Whitecloud
1935 — 2011

Crews repairing damaged train tracks

Alcohol is unloaded from a tanker punctured in a derailment

By LYNNE TERRY
THE OREGONIAN

Railroad officials worked nonstop cleaning up and repairing track damaged in the derailment and fire of a Portland & Western train that hit a tanker filled with denatured alcohol Wednesday.

Mike Williams, spokesman for Portland & Western's parent company Genesee & Wyoming, said the cleanup was expected to be completed sometime today, but the tracks probably would not be able to handle trains until at least Sunday.

BENJAMIN BRINK/THE OREGONIAN

About 20 workers, including representatives from the Oregon Department of Environmental Quality, the Oregon Department of Transportation, the Federal Railroad Administration and Railworks Track Systems looked over the wrecked train and burned lumber cars to determine how best to clean up the damage. The tracks could be closed to regular operations until at least Sunday, officials said. To see raw video of the fire from the Portland Fire Bureau, go to oregonlive.com/portland.

STUART TOMLINSON/THE OREGONIAN

About 50 workers and contractors continue cleanup and repairs on the Portland & Western Railroad line north of Portland on Friday. An overheated wheel bearing caused the derailment Wednesday afternoon of a log-laden train, which then crashed into tankers carrying ethanol, setting them on fire.

Hot wheel bearing led to derailment

By STUART TOMLINSON
THE OREGONIAN

An overheated wheel bearing on a railcar transporting logs along U.S. 30 caused the train to derail this week, officials said Friday.

The defective wheel slid off the left side of the track and then tore into railroad ties, shredding them for 2½ miles until the car fell completely off the track and smashed into two tankers parked on a parallel side track, said Ron Russ, president and general manager of the Portland & Western Railroad.

Overheated bearings caused derailment

PORTLAND — A freight train derailment that set off a large fire along Highway 30 just north of Portland was caused by overheated wheel bearings on one of the rail cars.

A wheel bearing on a rail car loaded with logs caused the wheels on the train to tear up railroad ties for more than two miles before the Wednesday derailment, a Portland & Western Railroad manager said Friday.

The train hit a tanker car full of denatured alcohol and it ruptured, leading to an intense fire that took about three hours to put out and caused an evacuation in the area.

State and federal officials quickly checked to make sure it was an accident with no terrorist connection.

81300
81700
AMF
SP
THE

MYTH..

Woman injured by train in Eugene

A young woman was taken to a Springfield hospital after police say she was struck by a train early Thursday morning in Eugene.

The woman was heading home from a local tavern when she was hit by the Amtrak train near West Third Avenue and Lincoln Street just after midnight. Police said alcohol use may have contributed to the incident.

The woman has not been identified by police, who say she is in her 20s.

An ambulance dispatch log shows that medics took the woman to Sacred Heart Medical Center at RiverBend. The extent of her injuries is not known.

Freight trains to link Coos, Lane counties

COOS BAY — Freight trains could be running between parts of Coos and Lane counties by early June.

The World newspaper reported the Oregon International Port of Coos Bay hopes to get trains rolling between Reedsport and the community of Danebo soon.

Port spokeswoman Elise Hamner said full service could come by September.

The port has been the recipient of tens of millions of dollars in state and federal funding to restore rail service between Coos Bay and Eugene, which shut down in 2007.

One injured in accident with train

One person was injured and transported to a hospital Friday afternoon following an accident with a train in Eugene, according to the Eugene Fire Department.

The incident occurred just before 5 p.m. at West Third Avenue and Monroe Street. No other information was made available Friday.

Turner

Man dies after being found near railroad

A 25-year-old man found alongside railroad tracks five miles south of Turner in Marion County died after he was taken to a hospital Friday night.

A Union Pacific Railroad employee discovered Michael A. Birkinshaw lying by the tracks near Duckflat Road Southeast and Marion Hill Road Southeast and called 9-1-1.

Marion County sheriff's deputies and Turner Fire District personnel gave him first aid until he was taken to Salem Hospital for emergency treatment, where he died. An initial investigation indicates that Birkinshaw, whose last known address was in Berkeley, Calif., either jumped or fell from a southbound freight train, deputies said. They were unable to find anyone who witnessed the incident.

— Emily E. Smith

Sunday, March 27, 2011

Transient found near tracks dies at hospital

Man either jumped or fell from train south of Turner

Statesman Journal

An injured man found lying next to railroad tracks south of Turner on Friday night died at Salem Hospital, the Marion County Sheriff's Office said Saturday.

The man, identified as a transient whose last known address was in Berkeley, Calif., either fell or jumped from a southbound freight train, sheriff's spokesman Don Thomson said.

A Union Pacific Railroad worker spotted the man lying by tracks near Duckflat and Marion Hill roads SE and called 911 at 10:46 p.m. Friday, Thomson said. The area is about five miles south of Turner. The worker spotted the body while the train he was operating had stopped to allow another train to pass in the opposite direction.

The victim was identified as Michael A. Birkinshaw, 25, who lived a transient lifestyle. His mother in Idaho was contacted using a cellphone found near his body. Thomson said Birkinshaw had last spoken with her on or about March 16 and told her he was going to ride a train south.

Two seconds of horror under a train costs man, 23, his leg

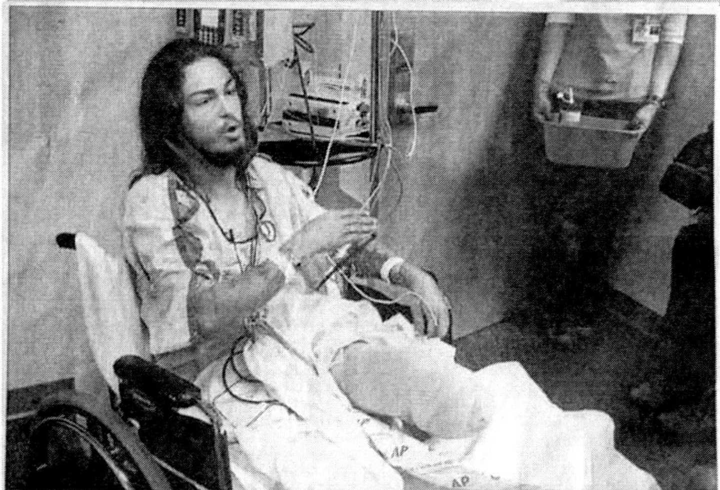

James Piles, 23, likened the pain of losing his left leg under the train to having a steel rod wrapped around his leg or being stepped on by an elephant. He said he wasn't under the influence of marijuana at the time. "I got hit because I was stupid, not because I was stoned," he said. "It was totally my fault."

Train severs leg of man near tracks

PORTLAND — A freight train severed the leg of a man walking through Portland on his way from the recent Rainbow Family gathering in Washington state.

James Piles, 23, said Tuesday at the hospital that he enjoys walking beside trains, but this time a car caught his backpack and spun him around.

The accident happened late Monday.

Piles said he wound up beneath the train, and knew the instant it happened that he'd lost his leg. His left leg was cut just below the knee.

James Piles was snatched walking beside the tracks, but says the ordeal won't end his life on the road

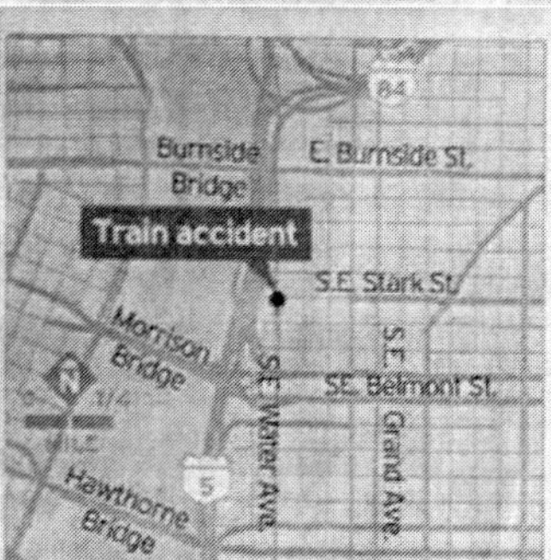

DAVID BADDERS/THE OREGONIAN

By LYNNE TERRY
THE OREGONIAN

Nearly 15 hours after a train cut off his lower left leg, James Piles was wheeled out of an ICU unit at OHSU Hospital ready to talk about the experience.

The 23-year-old, tethered to a beeping monitor and drug-dispensing IV, recounted in a calm voice how he and a buddy were strolling next to train tracks near Southeast Water Avenue and Stark Street on Monday evening. They'd just been back in Portland two days, after visiting the Rainbow Family gathering in the Gifford Pinchot National Forest in Washington. Heading south, a locomotive came from behind them, passing on their right.

"I heard it," Piles said. "I was walking right next to it.

The train hit the green army-style bag Piles totes on his back, stuffed with a sleeping bag and other gear for life on the road. He spun 270 degrees, he said, and was thrown under the dark train. As he crawled out, he said, the train severed his leg in a "nice clean cut."

"It was real quick — like two seconds," he said.

He crawled toward his leg, which

Please see TRAIN, Page B2

To see a video of James Piles describing how he fell beneath the wheels of a Union Pacific train, go to **oregonlive.com/portland**

had been flung about 15 feet. He tried to grab it but dropped it. He knew he had lost his leg for good.

"I was heartbroken and freaking out," he said. "It scared the bejesus out of me."

His friend, 22-year-old Asaiah Andrews, who was walking about 10 feet away holding his kitten, Ganja, witnessed the whole scene. First he saw blood on his friend's head and then a lower leg on the ground, boot still on, and a big pool of blood.

"I got hit because I was stupid, not because I was stoned," Piles said. "It was totally my fault."

He estimates the train was going 15 miles an hour.

Officials found signs of an accident a few cars back from the locomotive, Espinoza said.

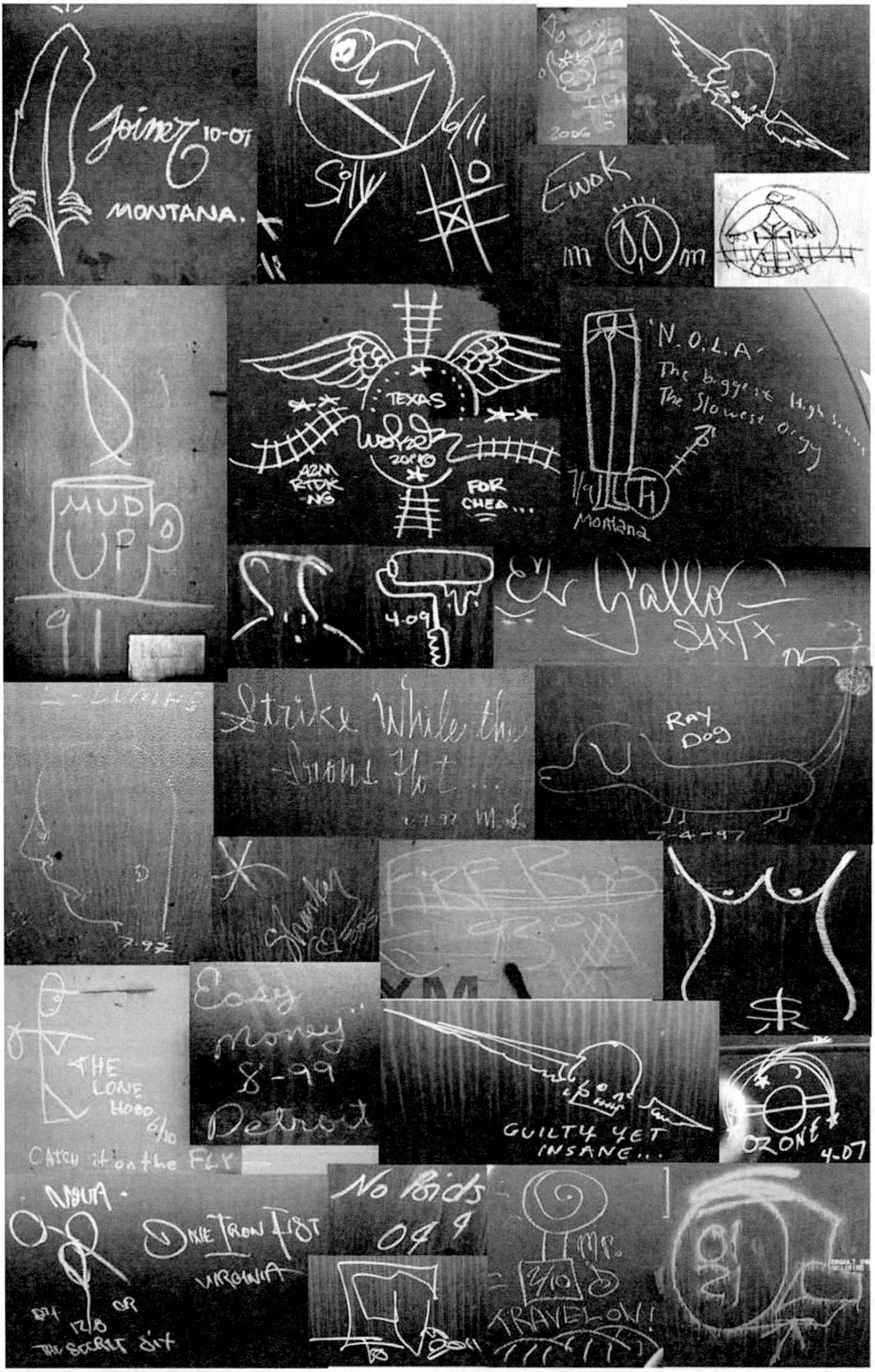
Joiner 10-07
MONTANA.
Silly
6/11
Ewok
TEXAS
A2M
RTDK
NS
FOR
CHEA...
'N.O.L.A'
The Slowest orgy
Montana
MUD
UP
4.09
El Gallo
SAxTX
Strike While the
Irons Hot...
RAY
DOG
7-92
THE
LONE
HOBO
6/10
CATCH it on the FLY
Easy
Money
8-99
Detroit
GUILTY YET
INSANE..
OZONE
4-07
No Kids
04
ONE IRON FIST
VIRGINIA
THE SECRET SIX
TRAVELON!

June 2011

Eugene, OR- *Aboard the sold-out #13 Coast Starlight. Destination: Seattle (if they don't first kick me off for not having a ticket) . . . Junction City . . . Harrisburg . . .* Under a thin gray-melding-to-blue-on-the-western-horizon sky, the cool, calm Willamette Valley is just starting to sallow with the demise of the rainy season and the start of some increasingly hot weather. This valley, the Valley of Sickness, is chock-full of enough allergens and pollens to make most out-of-towners look as if they've been profusely crying, especially in the summer . . . *Acres and acres of idle pastures . . . strange coniferous knobs and unpredictable juts of earth protruding to the foothills of the Cascades . . . one-lane country roads cross the tracks and bisect fields of hay cut and perfectly aligned for easy baling . . . corrugated-metal buildings with their backs to the tracks and factories with pallets stacked stories high . . . Sheep graze, marked with colored denotation . . . spur-tracks branch off into vacant lots where abandoned trailer-homes and ruined cars sit . . . Piles of uprooted ties . . . Scrap-metal and trash gondolas transporting these exhausted ties . . . Empty lumber racks . . . Albany . . . Portland and Western . . . Willamette and Pacific's yard winds behind the army-base size Weyerhauser factory as I-5 parallels to my right, a snowcap crest faintly visible deep in the Cascades . . . Gasoline billboards and WIDE LOAD-homes built to be loaded up and moved by flatbed truck . . . Encroaching hills and lone country roads . . . greenhouses cheaply constructed under plastic and rebar . . . Trackside trees blur by . . . Horse pastures and equines and dark soil tilled and being watered . . . Tiny Marion . . . Duckflat Road . . . Driveways trailing back into secret estates . . . A freshly planted plot with one of those airport hangar-looking things across it . . . Tree-lines separate fields idle and unplanted and overgrown and in all different stages of agricultural growth . . . PVC pipe running the length of a field through rusty, spoked wheels in order to be easily transported . . . Lumber mills (more) . . . Salem (Marion County), ball fields, campuses, Main Street through the state's capital, black Labradors riding in the back of a white pickup truck . . . Labish . . . Junk yards and gravel lots and loading docks . . . More acres of grass and alfalfa and all matter of crops, bisected by two-digit roadways . . . Mt. Hood appears on the NE horizon . . . Gervais and Woodburn . . . sided hoppers and grainers . . . a cemetery and an overpass . . . more greenhouses and the frames of future greenhouses . . . Rolling hills shadow the tracks . . . Canby: shopping outlets . . . Off-white and gray train cars whizzing by . . . A densely wooded area that contains homes high above the snaking Willamette River . . . Boats exploring the sandy beaches . . . Coalca- steep cliffs of rock and boulder and dense green woods and a matching green marsh . . . the southbound Amtrak, our sister train . . . The river wide .*

tanks southbound!

COAST STARLIGHT ROUTE MAP and SYMBOLS

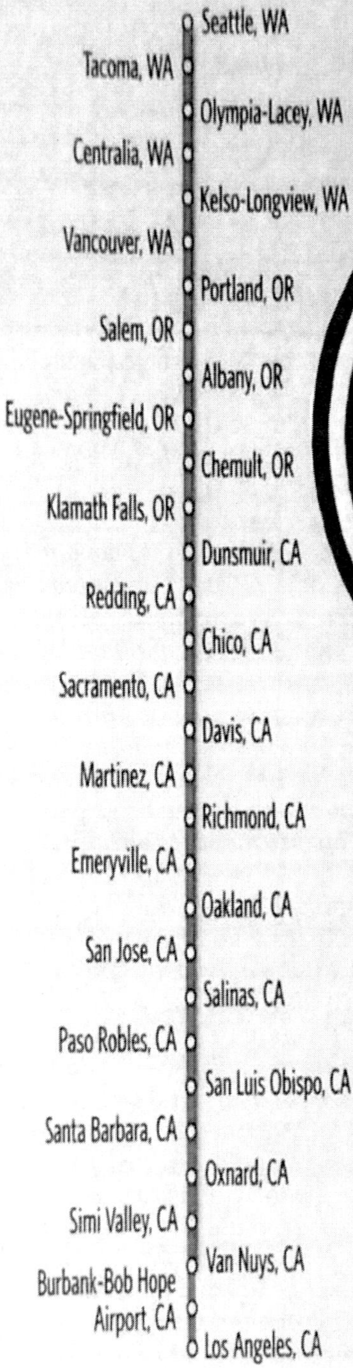

. . Corrugated-metal barn-like structures . . . Jet skies and boats on the water . . . houseboats afloat with wooden docks . . . the great industrialized version of Willamette Falls with its surrounding, shuttered industry and cesspools of flotsam-and-jetsam . . . Looking down and out over rooftops in Oregon City . . . Above, a northward-migrating, entropizing flying-V . . . Gladstone, the sky still a smoky gray . . . Clackamas River . . . Valleys within the Valley . . . Willsburg Junction . . . A golf course bordering Brooklyn yard . . . the inbounds of Portland—high, futuristic overpasses and 19th Century trestles . . . The river high, people everywhere on the move, walking across Steel Bridge, biking, jogging, acclimating to the muggy summer climate . . . (Once I get past Portland I'll be fine, but I'm worried about the forty-minute layover) . . . [Forty minutes later-the train departs Portland on time.] The National Railway Historical Society filed into the nearly-empty viewing car that I remained in during the layover and it's now more than I didn't pay for, a veritable tour the entire sub from Portland to Seattle . . . *through northwest Portland and BNSF's Lake Yard (which I don't too often get to see) bordered by Forest Park . . . across the Willamette*

Mt. Hood over Columbia River

River . . . into a deep shady ravine with high bridges . . . across the Columbia Lieu to Hayden Island, then across the wide Columbia River with Mt. Hood glistening on the eastern horizon . . . Into Washington State . . . through Vancouver's BNSF yard of tankers and hoppers and maroon stock of varying sorts, great white BNSF autoracks, engine shops . . . At the north end sit outbound and inbound trains . . . BNSF and CN galore zooming by both sides of the viewing car . . . Vancouver Lake peeking through the trees . . . Felida . . . Houseboats on the Lake River . . . The Ridgefield Wildlife Refuge and tiny Ridgefield itself—native Chinookan land . . . Cattle graze across the water on matted yellow pastures . . . Lewis River . . . The train runs in between north and southbound traffic on the I-5 interstate and an Amtrak Cascades passes south . . . The Columbia River reappears with an eddying surface which denotes current and significant depth . . . Kalama—a grain port with two totem poles, one being a 140-foot-tall western red cedar . . . Log yards and lumber industry all over, BNSF maroon-hoppers stretching and winding away from the mainline for miles . . . Osprey nesting atop dock piers . . . I-5 now to the east, cradled by healthy green conifers not lessened in vibrancy by the colorless sky . . . Kelso/Longview covered in Mt. St. Helen's ash . . . Cowlitz River lumber towns . . . The riverbank an elongated pile of ballast . . . Empty well-cars . . . an old, long, wooden trestle impressive in its architecture off to the right . . . The 1,165-foot-long Ostrander Tunnel through Rocky Point—the first tunnel on the Seattle sub . . . Toutle River . . . A landscape of volcanic ash from the great eruption of 1981 . . . a metal trestle crossing the Cowlitz River . . . Olequa Creek . . . Little Falls—now called Vader . . . The concave statue of Mt. St. Helens marking the eastern horizon . . . Palmer . . . Centralia . . . Lush green rushing by on all sides, the hazy sky overhead a matte of light grays and off-whites . . . Mima Mounds- low, circular, domelike mounds on the prairie that have perplexed geologists for centuries . . . East Olympia Junction—Mt. Rainier forty-something miles to the northeast with a 14,000-plus-foot apex jutting raggedly into the sky . . . Lacy station . . . Rolling high across the Nisqually River on elevated tracks with empty containers strewn along on the ballast . . . another Cascades passes south as this train spans both I-5 and the Nisqually River Delta and merges east onto tracks alternately routed to Tacoma

Mt. Rainier

Don't Try It!

. . . Grasping the southeastern shore of the insanely deep Puget Sound, snowy Olympic Mountains to the west . . . boats and piers . . . The Sound looking not unlike the Columbia River . . . A links golf course . . . more rivers and bridges . . . Tacoma Narrows, where the Sound becomes a little less than a mile wide and is spanned by a suspension-bridge that replaced Galloping Gertie, the original suspension-bridge that in November 1940 suddenly collapsed four months after its construction due to a kind of mystical aerostatic fluttering (a self-feeding and potentially destructive phenomenon where aerodynamic forces on an object couple with the structure's natural mode of vibration to produce rapid periodic motion, an example of elementary forced resonance.: If the energy input by the aerodynamic exitation in a cycle is larger than that dissipated by the damping in the system, the amplitude of vibration will increase, resulting in self-exciting oscillation) *. . . The 4,400-foot-long Nelson-Bennet tunnel underneath Point Defiance . . . Into a much shorter tunnel . . . Tacoma . . . Commencement Bay . . . Puyallup River . . . More bridges and rivers and mostly empty tracks . . . A forty-four car BNSF southbound . . . Meeker . . . Miles upon miles of quadruple inbound-tracks stuffed mostly with empty, waiting-to-be-used well-cars . . . Bonus, Huge, Erupto, Kaput, Boans . . . Seattle.*

Seattle, WA

Olympia

Train kills woman from Olympia area

An empty grain train struck and killed a woman Wednesday night in east Olympia, a Burlington Northern Santa Fe spokesman said.

Authorities say the 34-year-old woman, who was not immediately named, was from the Olympia area.

BNSF spokesman Gus Melonas said four freight trains were held temporarily while railroad officials and local authorities investigated.

The train that hit the woman originated at Kalama, Wash., and was bound for Grand Forks, N.D.

— The Associated Press

Seattle

Slow-moving train derails

A freight train derailed early Tuesday as the result of a low-speed collision at a BNSF Railway switching yard beside Airport Way South at Boeing Field.

A train carrying domestic cargo and going 5 mph failed to stop and struck a train carrying double-stacked international cargo where two tracks converge,

There were no injuries and no damage to the track. BNSF teams from Seattle and Pasco rerailed the two segments at 4:30 p.m., Melonas said.

NORTHWEST

Amtrak train strikes truck near Vancouver

VANCOUVER, Wash. — One person was taken to the hospital Monday after an Amtrak train hit a pickup truck at a private crossing six miles east of Vancouver.

Pedestrian killed by freight train

SEATTLE — A male pedestrian was struck and killed after he reportedly ran in front of a loaded coal train in Seattle Sunday.

The automatic warning devices were functioning properly and the train was sounding its horn, a Burlington Northern Santa Fe spokesman said.

Witnesses told train officials that the man ran in front of the train.

The train was traveling at about 22 miles per hour and was heading to Roberts Bank, B.C., from Montana.

The man was taken to a local hospital where he was pronounced dead. Trains were released at 4:30 p.m. Sunday.

Vancouver

Man, 69, injured in train-vehicle crash

A 69-year-old man was taken to an area hospital Monday evening after an Amtrak train struck a vehicle in Vancouver.

Four of the 14 cars that derailed late Saturday were tankers that each contained 15,000 gallons of lye, a chemical used as a drain cleaner and for other purposes.

Mudslides block railroad tracks

SEATTLE — Three mudslides in Washington knocked out rail service on lines south and north of Seattle.

Two of the slides on Sunday occurred near Everett, Burlington Northern Santa Fe officials said.

One of the slides hit Sunday morning and buried one of the two BSNF main line tracks.

Also near Everett on Sunday, another train hauling intermodal containers from Chicago struck a slide that impacted a line north of Seattle.

A third slide occurred between Ridgefield and Felida, near Vancouver. Passenger operations were suspended for 48 hours starting at 1 p.m. Sunday.

Heavy rain caused more than 20 incidents for rail officials in Washington this winter.

Derailment cleanup may take weeks

SEATTLE — A railroad spokesman said Sunday that it might take three weeks to remove all debris from the site where a freight train derailed and sideswiped another on the banks of Puget Sound, spilling a small amount of a hazardous chemical.

Last Minute Kid 5.10
ROLL ON COLUMBIA!
DIX
9-09
The Iron Pelican
IMPENDING DOOM
WOK
Dan Nowhere 8/10
this'll get to chi-town way before me
708
CAR DEPT
Etaja 05/27/10
TG
BAD THINGS MAN
GET-IN-
FIT-IN....
....RIGHT
30-5-11
0209
310
R.I.P. A-LORGE

Seattle

Olympic Mountains

June 2011

Seattle, WA- Balmer yard was a no-go. Whisky and Aware showed up with our friend the Baby Samoan and we waited there on the tracks opposite a little-league outfield fence throwing rocks and shooting small boulders and golf balls at empty beer bottles with a sling shot and watching the balls careen wildly off whatever it hit and fly back at us like from a pitching machine, or bounce astray and hit a train that would then echo across the tracks with that hollow metal sound. A doublestack came on the mainline several hours after dark and rolled steadily through the yard. A super-long hotshot with three front units and two rear DPUs: the Cadillac of freight trains—the one we had been waiting for—a dream ride destined for the highline east. It slowed near the end giving us that kind of false hope that makes you pack up your stuff just in case you might actually be able to catch the thing on the fly, but when you get close enough you realize there never really was a chance and Freddy buzzes past and blinks off into the distance leaving you miffed and frustrated at the blatantly missed opportunity. A line of maroon hoppers (empty, I know from walking past them earlier in the afternoon at the grain mill along the bay) ticked to life, but with no DPU I was not convinced. And so with the Baby Samoan still around, we decided to accept his offer to drive us over to the main IM yard in Seattle—Stacy—and we found it right off the freeway with no problem. He dropped us off right by a big Home Depot where there should be

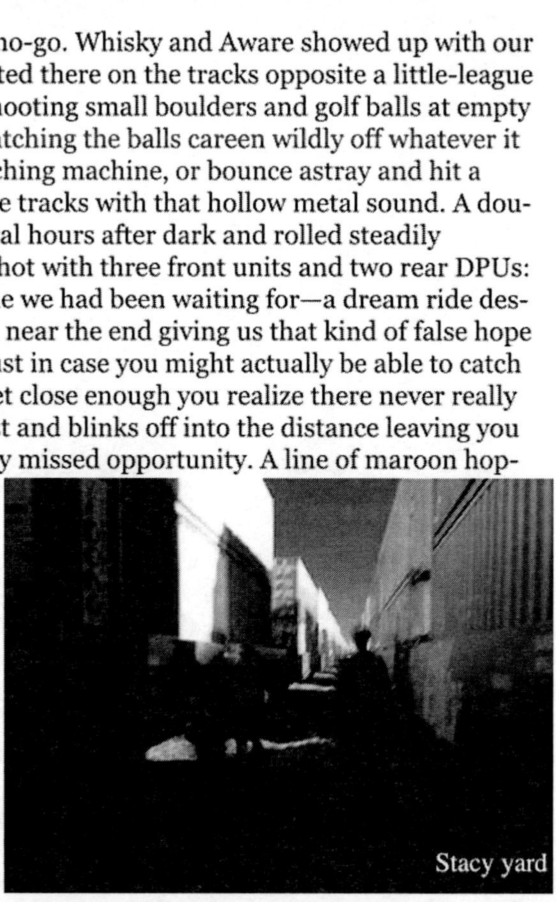

Stacy yard

-Balmer yard- Seattle, WA

Stacy yard and Seattle

a big fence blocking access to the sensitive freight yard but there's not, and we hopped in between lines and walked down one of the jeep-paths to check if either of the two long, loaded lines there had a DPU or front units or a Freddy to tell us which direction they were headed. We ended up camping off to the side of the yard behind some shed-like factory building where big wooden spools were turned on their sides like tables and there stood a basketball goal. I bedded down in a gravel lot next to some employee parking spaces and slept surprisingly well despite all-night train horns and engines passing close enough to wake me.

The morning presented sunshine and the first blue sky in days, but unfortunately clouded over again before long. Stacy Yard appeared much more intimidating without the shadow of night, and except for a line of mixed rolling stock that pulled into the yard, the layout looked the same as the night before. I strolled past the yard office to take a gander and finally saw the scope of the yard from its interior being longer and much, much larger than I had thought, and harboring a much more diverse rolling stock—not just IMs and well-cars. On my way out a BNSF cop, who had been on the other side of the yard waiting for me to cross the tracks, rolled up after I did not cross the tracks and instead started across the employee parking lot toward the road. He put his sirens on, drove over, and told me to Step in front of the car please, Sir.

"You a railfan?"

"Yes."

"Then you should know th-blah blah blah..."

"Well I didn't really know where I-blah blah..."

I told him I had just ridden the Amtrak up from Portland and was only taking pictures.

"Sounds good," he said.

He took my ID and ran it and then gave it back and told me to hit the road so we said Fuck Stacy! and headed north via the Hwy to try and catch-out of Everett instead.

*

Everett, WA 12or1300- I was all wrong about Everett from the start. There are two yards in town, but I didn't have a map to look at, only my CC. Delta yard is a one-sided, decently large switching yard on the east side of town. 16th St. dead-ends right at its south throat, and that's how we found it. But having never before been here, I was directionally confused. Looking straight out over the yard is clearly an eastward view of the Cascades, which means eastbound trains must depart Delta yard either geographically north or geographically south. However, trains coming from Seattle run north along the Sound then make a u-turn to come through Everett, passing through neither Delta or Bayside—the other yard. But, I thought Bayside, which sits opposite Delta, on the west side of town, I

PORT OF EVERETT
OFFICE (425) 259-3164
EMERGENCY (425) 238-4460
UP THE CRUST
HESH
F.O.A.D

thought Bayside yard was actually north of Delta yard, across the slough, and that all trains on the Scenic sub *had* to pass through Bayside in order to go east, and then cross the Snohomish River slough on a single-track bridge that splits off in three directions, (1) through the westside of town where the Amtrak station is, (2) straight into the funnel of the Delta yard, or (3) bypassing the yard east on one of three tracks (two of which are today occupied by head-less IM trains). The difficulty is, with the way Everett is laid out and the tracks running north/south, directions are doubly difficult to get straight. But my intuition tells me that eastbound trains depart GEO southbound, and after consulting a generic map I tore from a phonebook at a nearby market, I eventually had to draw it out in the sand on the bank of the bay to explain this reasoning to my traveling cohort . . . *We've been all around Delta yard, from the north throat where we hopped a fence and walked down an overgrown service road through tall weeds that exacerbated everyone's allergies but then still couldn't get to the tracks because of a muddy marsh-like area and instead had to just cut our losses and retreat more worn-down than before, to the south throat where we followed a path to investigate the catch-out potential from under the freeway, over to the east side where inter-models are loaded and where the yard is heavily fenced off, all the way back to the west side where a gravel plateau lends access to trains but not advantage. We eventually came to sit under a bridge on the northwest side of the yard, looking east to distant pinnacles of snow with the sky above dark and parasitic, waiting for activity in the yard to quell (an IM to quit working and go ahead and kill itself, and a white SUV to return from north of the yard) so we can make our way down and across the yard and up to the train bridge that crosses the slough, where the plan is to essentially choke the train off when it crosses the bridge and catch it on the fly and get the hell out of Everett to kickstart this trip . . .*

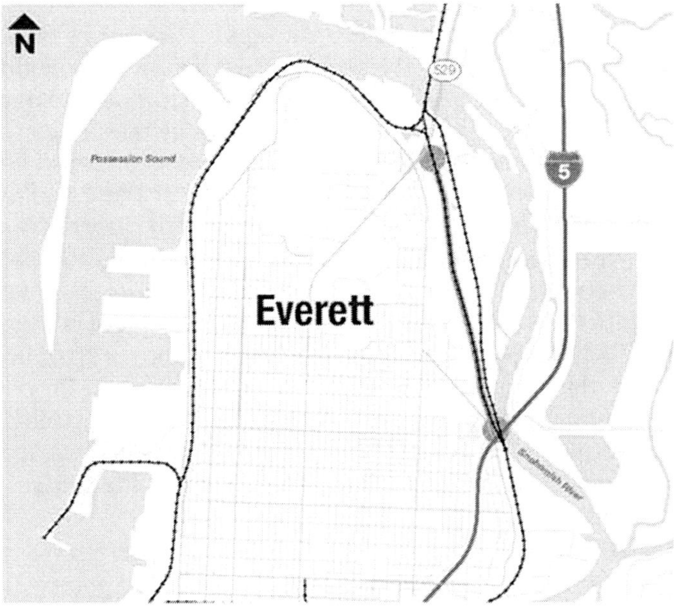

The first sign that we were in a good catch-out spot was Old

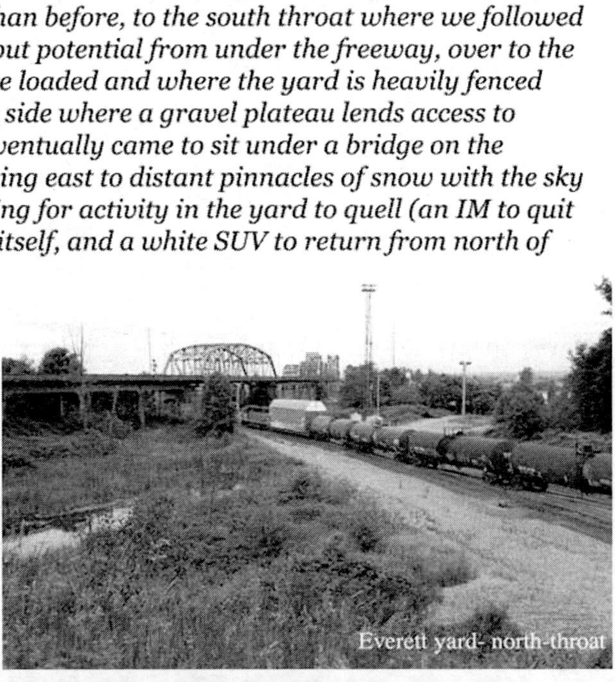
Everett yard- north-throat

Crow. There were two Old Crow tags on the pillars right where we waited and I knew right then that if he'd been here before and caught-out then we'd be alright. We walked down to the bay and set our stuff behind one of the pillars where we could view the low-lying tracks that bridge the slough . . . *Miserable conditions in Everett . The mosquitoes are as bad by this brackish bay as I've ever seen in the Pacific Northwest (which happens to be at Waldo Lake in the Oregon Cascades). The tide is quickly coming in so we have to resort to higher, more visible ground to stay dry, and Whisky and Aware are having the worst allergies possible—all red-eyed, sneezing, and blowing whale spouts of snot out alternating nostrils . . .* From the west side of Everett a northbound general manifest with three BNSF units rolled slowly across the bridge we were preying on, providing insight into the direction of future trains and confirming, at least for now, my theory that trains cross the bridge slow enough to catch on the fly . . . *As Aware lays out his self-inflating air mattress to take up some rest while we wait, a southbound coal train suddenly comes rolling 6-mph across the bridge. Fuck yes!*

June 2011

Spokane, WA 0900- We made good time getting here last night after finally catching-out of Everett on empty coal-car porches. We caught the train on the fly after it crossed the slough, veering sharply left of Delta yard and passing under Hwy 2 all rickety and slow like it was going to stop any given time. It was filthy too, and my hand somehow got cut and began bleeding as I hunched over uncomfortably so that my head didn't hit the slanted metal overhang of the (half)suicide porch. Just south of the yard the train altogether clanked to a halt and I saw Aware, who had been three or four porches ahead of me, scamper off the train-literally scamper—up a gravel hill off into the brush. As Whisky followed suit it became obvious they were running from what could only be one thing, and I quickly and half-assedly grabbed my shit and ran too, looking back under the train for some sign of the Bull. They had both seen him sitting under the bridge there, as if waiting for someone to arrive. We laid there in the weeds on the backside of a hill, but within a minute the train clanked back together and clamored on forward, and I thought we should stay with the train so we all ran back out and climbed on again, this time with me ahead of them on porches.

The train continued on unsteadily, passing a truck where a female worker stood at a track-switch, and as she very blatantly saw me on the train dribbling slowly by, all I could do was wave. The train pulled up a few hundred yards more and stopped on a lower-level track just outside of Everett where the tracks re-converge with the west-side-of-town tracks, and as the train sat there we all walked the line back toward the DPU. I cut through tall, thick weeds to the higher mainline and, cautious of other trains or trucks

southbound along the Snohomish

riding on the rails, walked back at least ninety cars to where two giant BNSF units were idling—one, the orange and black design, and the other, the older green and white scheme. Whisky and Aware had already boarded the first unit, and after taking a horse-bath with a crew-pack I took to the second unit and laid on the floor and read.

DPU departing Everett

An hour later I heard the radio in the cab squalk to life. The Engineer's voice came in saying that the Inbound Crew had just boarded and that the southbound empty coal train [our train] was ready to depart, but that the Outbound Crew had reported a couple of quote Trespassers in the DPs (not DPUS, but I assume it means the same). A dispatcher then responded with confirmation that Yes, he had called and reported the Outbound-Crew's claim to the Police, but whether or not They, the Police, got down there to quote Take care of that, he did not know. "Okey Dokey," the Engineer replied with an implied shrug of his shoulders. He went on to say that the southbound empty coal train was, regardless, ready to depart.

Never before have I had the benefit of a forewarning to my own possible arrest. I ran frantically to tell Whisky to pack up his stuff and be on the lookout, but just then the train began hissing furiously, steaming out its side, and pulled forward . . . *1 mph . . . 2 mph . . .* We soon came to realize what had happened was that someone else must have already been in the DPU, and that when the train stopped where the Bull was sitting under the bridge, it was to pull whoever-was-on-the-DPU off, not us. We realized this because Aware had found a left-behind water bottle upon entering the DPU, and we were now rolling. So what a coincidence that we were spared a charge by catching-on to suicide-porches instead of straight onto the DPU . . . *Veering SSE along a green valley of yellow daisies with coniferous mountains rising against the glowing, dusk-laden west and the sky above looking like it is any minute going to storm . . . Our trajectory becomes more apparent as the tracks arc subtly eastward and larger mountains close in and the glow of the setting sun becomes positioned directly behind the train. Thick wisps of cumulus drape the foothills of the Washington Cascades like giant smoky dragons hovering between the uplift crevices . . . The train hugs tightly to the winding path of the Skykomish, a river fed by forest snowmelt and rainfall, full and roiling through towns like Monroe, Sultan, Start Up, and tiny Goldbar, where a friend of mine just last week stayed while visiting her sister at school . . . Darkening forests, dense and lush and Rain Forest-like green, shaded from sunlight, the forest floor a reverse canopy of downed logs and pine needles and felled branches . . . The train climbs up and into a light rain that does not so much as fall as it does just hang in the air and appear on the cab's windshield, slowly obscuring frontward vision as elevation becomes higher and higher . . . Rolling on a lone rail-trail through the rugged Cascades that no road comes close to taking, the train crosses the Skykomish a dozen*

Crossing the Skykomish

DPU-barreling at dusk

seperate times on increasingly steep and impressive trestles a tall-tree's height over deep ravines of frothy, tumbling streams. BNSF's Scenic Subdivision is just that, even more-so than the Oregon Cascades, and the tracks eventually plunge ruthlessly into the Cascade Tunnel . . .

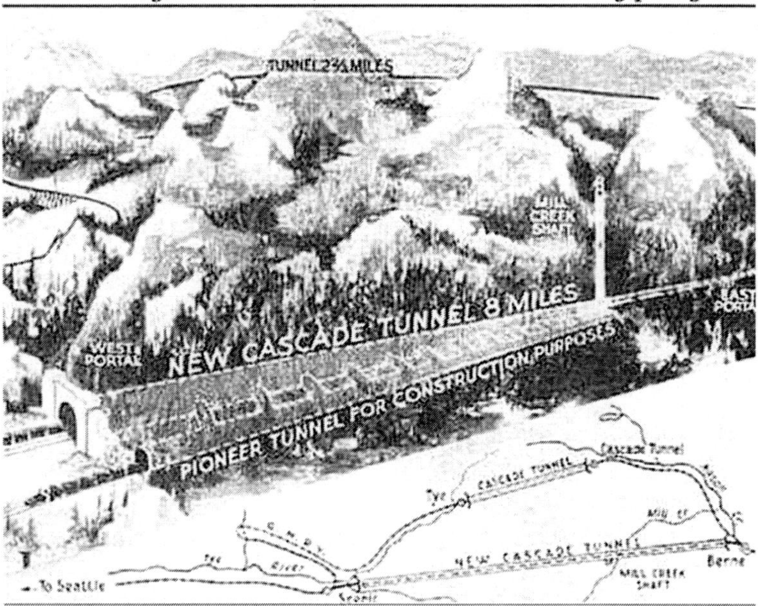

At 7.79-miles long—seriously!—BNSF's Cascade Tunnel is easily the longest hole of any railroad in the country, receiving only mild competition from UP's Norden Tunnel (see *Railroad Semantics #4*) and outdone by only a more-complex tunnel in British Columbia (not yet explored). The 85-year-old Cascade Tunnel runs 1,180-feet below the Cascades Mountains of Stevens Pass, which was founded by "legendary" surveyor John Frank Stevens, who also discovered Maria Pass in the Rocky Mountains of Montana (and who also engineered the Panama Canal!). Stevens discovered the pass at the headwaters of Nason Creek in 1890 while working for Great Northern Railway. Six-years-of-construction-later the pass opened but it was not the final say in the railroad's routing. While relatively quick compared with the obstacles it faced, the construction of tracks across Stevens Pass was basically a big mess in the haste of underdeveloped techonology, complete with derailments, deaths, and train wrecks. Another, shorter tunnel was originally used near the top of the pass requiring no less than eight switchbacks, but Stevens Pass never really coalesced until the opening of the new Cascade Tunnel in 1929. Today, the original sections of track along with the abandoned first-tunnel scatter the mountains around Stevens Pass, and many have been restored and converted into hiking trails.

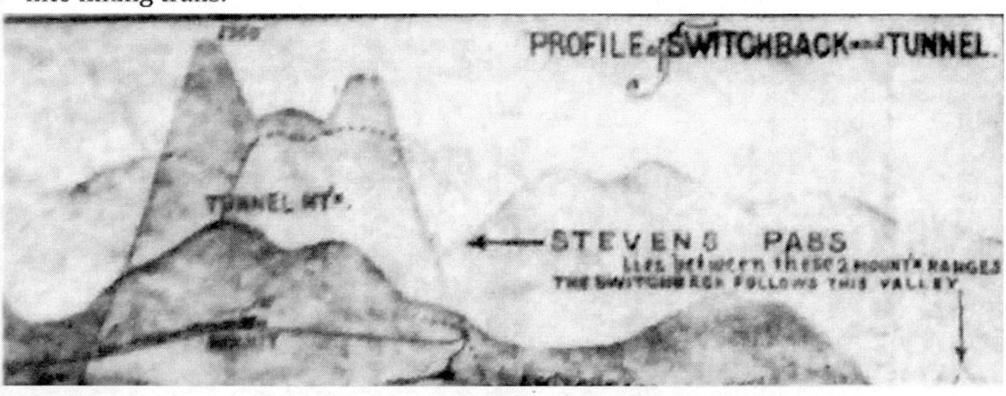

With a 25-mph speed limit, the Cascade Tunnel is limited to 28 trains a day due to its superior length, but which is a lot of damn trains! The tunnel was initially electrified and did not require ventilation, but since the use of diesel engines took

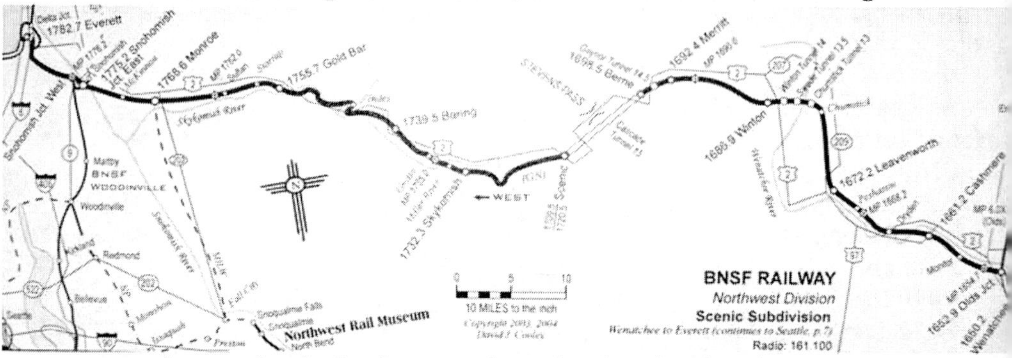

over around 1944, that had to be re-evaluated. What developed is interesting: once a train enters the tunnel, a door at the east entrance closes and an enormous snow plow-like fan blows cool air into the tunnel to help alleviate pressure problems and dissolve fumes. Then, as the train nears the exit, the fan shuts off and the door opens. Once the train has cleared the tunnel, the door closes again, the fan comes back on, and there's a thirty-minute rest period to clear the air before any other train can come through. And this is the case with both east and westbound trains. However Amtrak, which does use the tunnel on a daily basis, does not require this ventilation procedure.

Considering asphyxiation, an eastbound train is the more dangerous to be aboard as the tunnel has a 1.7% incline west-to-east and much more fuel is needed to power the tonnage uphill, therefore creating that much more exhaust than would a westbound train easing down the grade. But after so long in the hole it becomes meaningless to think of it this way. It's hard to say how long our train was actually engulfed in exhaustial blackness, but by the last mile or two the speed seemed to be about 15 or 20 mph—not fast—and because it was late and there really wasn't much to look at, I tended to lay on the floor breathing slowly with my face in my shirt as the fumes unmistakably infiltrated the cab's interior (perhaps I should have turned the air conditioner off too). I have serious doubts I could've survived the tunnel with merely a wet rag in some boxcar or hopper cubbyhole, but certainly not on a coal-car porch, which would have been certain death by carbon-monoxide poisoning. How others have done it, I'm not sure. I've heard of people filling trash bags with air, but even then you're risking that there will be enough air to last until the end.

It stood dark all around except for the faint bluish glow of the cab's monitor illuminating the ceiling, and every 1,500-feet a crossover to a parallel access tunnel

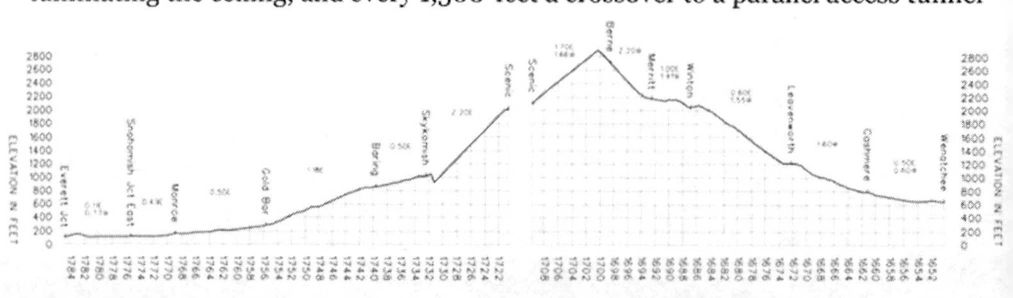

would flash by with dim yellow lights fanning across the cab. I could then look out the back window and see the outline of the tunnel lit dimly in the hazy, stirring exhaust of the train . . . *In the middle of what could only be the 8-mile Cascade Tunnel and I'm lying comfortably on the unit's floor staring sleepily up at the dim blue from the unit's monitor on the ceiling, listening to the cacophonous hum of the engine reverberating off the sooty tunnel walls. The sound has changed audibly from the normal engine's-roar to a roar very much contained and lacking Doppler effects as it repeatedly pummels the hollow archway. Every quarter mile there seems to be like an emergency area with a light, and the light zooms by and I can see out the back windshield. It's only vaguely starting to smell like exhaust in the unit, but otherwise OK . . .*

high in the Cascades

Once the train emerged I opened both windows to get a draft through the cab and stepped outside to breathe in fresh mountain air. The train slowed on the mainline as I laid back down, and with communicative precision stopped lengthwise beside a WBD hotshot, aligning the empty-coal-train's rear DPUs [the one's we were in] with the hotshot's front engine. I sat up to see what was going on and heard the front door of the cab open. A cautious worker looked inside and offered a friendly Hello, as if he was expecting someone.

"Oh, I'm not going to say anything," he said, stepping into the cab. "As long as you don't touch anything."

He reached behind me not for the inspection card but to turn the front lights of the DPU on, then exited.

"Take it easy," he told me, before, "Oh... and you didn't see me." : The unspoken Conductor-code of rails had been spoken again.

*

I clocked back in at dawn when Aware, who had come running down the catwalk across his unit to mine wearing only his black boxer shorts and a t-shirt, burst into my cab like a little kid on Christmas morning. I didn't even think we were yet to Wenatchee, but Whisky, who couldn't much sleep because his allergies were so bad that his nose was clogged up and he couldn't breath out his nostrils (he would have for sure had a deadly time riding stock through the Cascade Tunnel!),

Whisky quickly set me straight, reporting that Wenatchee signs had hours ago rolled by by the dozen. Sure enough we were soon crossing bridges and trestles above an Eastern Washington forest glazed in morning fog, overlooking concrete bridges that held the highway leading to Spokane.

early-morning-Washington forest

The empty coal train rolled clear across the city before stopping briefly to allow us to climb off and scamper down the ballast to Sprague Ave. where we ran into some kid who told us he had been sitting at the Flying J for hours trying to get a ride to Oregon and that there was nothing for him anymore in Spokane except the drugs and getting high and that we were on the biggest stripper-street in all of Spokane and that he was surprised there weren't more hookers out prowling. It was six-thirty in the morning.

*

1412- Spokane, old FTRA stomping-ground and a central hub for train hopping in the Pacific Northwest, was founded by Great Northern Railway in 1871. Originally called Spokane Falls, after a falls on the Spokane River where the native Spokane Indians fished, it is hence named for the Natives, a name that means Sun People. Our bright morning had the same effect as the rest of Washington, and clouded over again before noon so thick that I did not know where the sun sat in the sky but otherwise served as a good backdrop for photographs.

Collectively we made our way to the east side of town, which is more sprawled than I remembered/mental-mapped it to be. (If it was just I, I would've gladly just waited downtown, around Amtrak, but since I am traveling with two others, I have to account for them too.) We planned to catch a train on the CC, and the first set of tracks we came to on Fancher St., by a Home Depot and Costco-shopping complex, opened to a small yard where we sat and waited but soon became visually accosted by the presence of a white SUV. Everyone became uneasy. I went to explore the terrain and realized something was terribly wrong. Not only were there not enough trains here to justify it as Spokane's yard, but no traffic was coming through, and I *had* heard horns. Turns out the main Spokane yard is further down Fancher St., a half mile

Welcome to
Spokane
BigFoot
Dan Nowhere
8/09
DESERT RAT
UP THE CRUST
EBD
PPP TOUR 2011
NO TRESPASSING
Pocatello Paul 7 3 93
THE LONE HOBO
COWBOY ED 7·93
THE SALEM
8 BALL
Again Big Bubba
Big Bubba
F.R.A

wrong spot

or so, where the street elevates and bridges the tracks—that's the yard.

We gladly said Fuck Off to whomever that white SUV was and retraced our steps out and continued on down Fancher to the real yard, which runs at a slightly canted angle from where we were. It was all fenced off except for access on the south side through a gravel lot, and we sat outside the yard leaning against our packs, napping, and waiting for something to happen. There were, I could tell, several trains readying for departure, stretching for miles toward the city. The pillars under the bridge contained little to no spray paint but were mangled with decades of old hobo tags, including an enormous 1980s Coaltrain, as well as some old, early-90s FTRA insignia. I also saw the same "eastbound" streaks I had seen at the catch-out spot in Everett, on a silver box here in the Spokane yard written with the same blue marker.

Spokane yard

waking up trackside

June 2011

Spokane, WA 0800- I highly recommend, if you're in Spokane and have some time to kill or are looking for some place to go drink, the Checkerboard Tavern on East Sprague St. (good old Sprague!), which we happened upon in disheveled fashion after a near all-out-fiasco involving one of us being separated from the rest of the party—bags and all—a junk train going to Kettle Falls, and a BNSF Special Agent. The punk kids who run the Checkerboard—it's kind of a punk rock bar with a tinge of Spokane influenced skinheadism (I'm afraid), but still OK, and claims to have the longest running alcohol license in Washington State (since 1937)—the punk kids told us, over a very loud Circle Jerks record, that all the traveling kids they know get a ride twenty minutes or so east to Hauser, in Idaho, and catch-out there, and that that is the catch-out spot for all trains through Spokane. That would make sense because most of the trains we've seen just blow through and don't even slow on the mainline going through town. The punk kids said they bet they could even find us a ride out to Hauser, and in the meantime offered their backyard for us to sleep in and told us to come to their house for drinks later.

We had spent the entire afternoon in the Spokane train yard, and it was one of those days where the more time that elapses the more comfortable you feel trespassing around. We waited in three different spots trying to catch a through-train, but each train that came through hardly even slowed. We considered catching-out east to Whitefish (which would have actually been the right thing to do considering trains were CCing in Hauser), but remained diligent in our goal to not veer from the stated trajectory: south—get to Pasco, then head west to Wishram and on back to Portland (or maybe, if we're lucky, travel up the Deschutes River to Bend and continue on to Klamath Falls, then back up through the Cascades and Eugene to Portland).

We sat at some abandoned-building's back that had decade-old hobo scrawls

THE INSANE WINO
11-12-83
5-22-87
NO
TRESPASSING
THUNDER
WOMAN
NEW YORK
ANYWHERE THE
TRAIN GOING
7-4-86

JOHN
EAsley
SLIM
F.I.R.A
NO
TRESPASSING
NO
IRON GOD 93

carved into it, throwing rocks at cans and train cars and whatever else. Trains just kept blowing past on the mainline in both directions—lots of maroon-hopper lines but hotshots as well. Feeling more and more comfortable being there, I walked through the yard and found an MRL boxcar with both doors open on a line that sat hissing to move, and so we all clamored into it. Like I said, it was one of those days...

way too comfotable in Spokane

Whisky went out to draw on trains and was just about to mark a tanker, I could see, when "Hold it there, Partner!" came from outside the boxcar. I froze deadly silent and tip-toed back to the corner. This was no worker; a BNSF Special Agent had Whisky red-handed.

"Don't run," he warned pulling out his gun and pointing it right at Whisky's head while walking real slow toward him.

Whisky put his hands up turning his palms face out, and with only a camera around his chest said, "I'm only taking photographs," real dumb like.

Aware and I remained crouched and silent, knowing that if the Special Agent did not know we were in the boxcar, that Whisky'd not give us up. And smartly, so that the cop wouldn't find us, Whisky walked past the boxcar door to the Special Agent, who then turned him around, put him in handcuffs, and led him over the coupler to where his jeep sat on the gravel road.

on alert!

Aware and I were stuck in the boxcar with Whisky's bag and no idea what to do, and the train was now airing up to go. (If we climbed out into the yard we too would be arrested for trespassing, but if the train goes south then we'd be leaving Whisky behind in Spo-Compton with not even his phone or a sleeping bag.) With a piece of cardboard left in the boxcar, we draped it over us in the back corner as the train ticked to life.

[Meanwhile, Whisky stood on the jeep-path with the BNSF Special Agent discussing anti-terrorism efforts (the 10th anniversary of 9-11 was nearing), impressing the man with his poise, intellect, and natural charm, painting himself as prime railfan material by cooperating enthusiastically so that he would not be arrested. Apparently BNSF has an intricate computer system that keeps track of anyone stopped on BNSF railroad property and lists the location, date, and reason, along with what corrective action resulted. Whisky was certainly in that system, but it said he had only been stopped twice prior (when it was probably more like five or six times). The special agent called and checked those situations out, but Whisky had no warrants, and so this was Strike Three, an official citation, that which comprised a mandatory court appearance a month from now in none other than glorious Spokane, and an absence of which would warrant, well, a warrant.]

Whisky's finagled photo of the Special Agent

Minutes later—Aware and I were still extremely vulnerable, but all we could do was lay low—the train heaved air and began to pull out of the yard. Once it felt safe enough to peer out, it became obvious to us that the train was not a southbound like we had thought, and was not going back toward Wenatchee either, which we could have handled, but instead was heading north, toward Kettle Falls, and perhaps on into Canada from there—not the direction we needed to be heading. So while the train was still traveling at a manageable speed, we caught-off taking with us Whisky's bag, because if he was in jail we wanted to at least bail him out. I took a spill catching-off, a notebook fell out of Whisky's bag scattering an entire unbound CC guide all over the tracks, and I suddenly heard a hollering coming from behind me—someone else was on the train! I turned naturally to see who and to my utter disbelief saw Whisky hanging off a ladder, waving.

The reunion was a little unbelievable at first, like *Are you really here? Did we really just run back into each other?* As it turns out, since Whisky cooperated so well and really hadn't done anything more than Criminally Trespass taking photos, he received a rare pardon from the Special Agent and was let go with only as much as a verbal warning and the incident being reported in the BNSF system (which only BNSF authorities see, not city or state police). None of us could believe it. The Special Agent had assumed Whisky was just a serious railfan, even confiding that in all his eighteen-years as a rail cop only once had he ever encountered a railfan taking pictures in the middle of the train yard, and that was today. He had caught people in the train yard, of course, but those were the ones riding, he said. But never for a moment did he think that about Whisky because he, Whisky, carried no gear in which to hop a train and his accidental cover of only a camera made him seem a veritable railfan (a severely obsessed if not reckless one at that). And because the two times that Whisky had been stopped prior that came up in the BNSF system were merely for the same thing—trespassing whilst taking pictures—he was leniently let go.

After the special agent escorted him out of the yard, Whisky was then on his way to get a beer, naturally. He came to a gas station on Hyena Road that had a pay phone and tried to call his own cell-phone, which we were hoping he would.

However, as he was calling his phone, the train we were on began pulling out of the yard. Whisky suddenly saw the train from a distance, counted the units on front, and remembering the exact rolling stock realized it the same train; and so he dropped the phone off the hook and took off straight across the street like he was fleeing the Special Agent, ran through several parking lots, along the side of a building that was (thankfully) not fenced off, ran down into a ditch-like area, and then up a steep slope just as the very boxcar we were inside of passed in front of him, and he barely missed us. Thinking that we were most likely still aboard with his bags, Whisky caught-on to a back porch a dozen cars back and sat down. Looking off one side of the tracks he inadvertently caught a glimpse of someone walking away from the train, and it took a few moments for his subconscious to kick in before he familiarized my green Army pack and realized it was I. Hanging off the ladder as the train curved away from us, he sure enough saw Aware and I now walking away from the train after having just caught-off ourselves, and he hollered. If he hadn't been looking off that side of the train, this coincidence probably wouldn't have happened and he very well may have ended up in Kettle Falls with nothing while we would have been waiting outside the Spokane County Jail.

Spokane, WA

1320- It's a sunny day, partly cloudy with a bit of high wind, and my hand is bleeding in three different places with the skin peeled off my ring-finger knuckle from some obvious abrasion. My foot is bleeding also, from where the heel of my shoe has cut into it, and I feel like my hip is probably bruised from the fall. It all happened so fast, as it always does, and this time *I* am the one split up from the rest of the party.

We woke this morning beside the tracks somewheres near the Rainbow Room (also on Sprague), very near the exact place we climbed off the train the morning prior but now realizing that Yes, trains are not even stopping in Spokane to CC but must be doing so in Hauser, and that Spokane is just a clusterfuck of bad news for train-hoppers. We were headed back up the tracks to a creosote bridge I had seen from the train yesterday and that I have heard is a decent waiting spot, and came to an odd-angled track where a loaded GM train sat aired up and ready to go. It had only two units but the curious thing about that was that they were Union Pacific units. I had forgotten entirely that UP had its own trackage up to Spokane, and after a quick reference from my railroad atlas we crossed the street to catch-on to this soon-to-be-departing southbound train. A man talking on his cell-phone outside a random corrugated-metal office building became very excited about the prospect of us catching-out and sort of congratulated us, shaking each of our hands and telling us he had never before seen train-hoppers, which surprised me. By then the train had begun to move and not wasting any time we caught-on back-to-back porches . . . *this one has no porch! Get it! Get it!* . . . the front-facing one being just two cubbyholes on a big-belly grainer and the back one a gasket-side suicide porch that I took to. We rode the train through the crossing, past where we had slept, and into town, creeping through track switches and then stopping on one of two mainlines to wait for clearance. After an hour the train departed and rolled up a roller coaster-like incline on a high pillared bridge above the freeway west of town, then veered south on a sharp curve that lent an

heading south from Spokane on UP

incredible view of the now-obviously-very-long general-manifest train trailing back to a Spokane skyline being endlessly fed automobiles. Continuing south into a forested area, the train stopped on the single mainline and we all got off and walked back to more suitable porches—Whisky and Aware to one and me to my own, which I thought would be safer than traveling altogether on a single porch, visibility wise, but also so that if one person got spotted the others would not necessarily be fucked as well. Twenty minutes ticked by before the train moved again and rolled past two workers standing by a white truck, one of whom very blatantly saw me. The train crept by so slowly that the man turned his head catching my eye and very nonchalantly asked How's it going?

...just bailed

The train seemed as if it were loaded much too heavy, creeping along at walking speed, the ties underneath creaking like an old wooden floor. I quickly caught-off the opposite side and let about forty cars roll past before catching back on to a different porch, half the line back. The train crept on several more clicks and then stopped again for an hour-long nap in the sun. The next time it jerked into motion, it did so with increased push, as if DPUs had been put on the rear. My hopper then passed a white SUV that parked facing the train, and before I knew it that white vehicle was driving on the dirt service road right alongside the very porch I was riding. And to make the situation worse, the train was now pulling onto a siding to stop. *I* was fucked. But suddenly, for some reason, and maybe it was luck, the white SUV slowed ever-so-slightly, I noticed through a hole in the floor. I climbed out and peered off the side to make sure, and with that little bit of time afforded, I scrambled my stuff together in an armful and, again caught-off the opposite side of the train on the fly, which stranded me between a steep ravine and the train rolling about 10 mph a foot or so from my face. But I lost him. And as the white SUV kept driving I could only think of how to stay with my cohort. Three DPUs now approached, but they were BNSF units. Still, I caught on the first unit thinking that if there were workers aboard they'd be in the rearmost unit, but I walked right in on an ugly middle-age Engineer with glasses and a serious butt-broom.

down in Marshall Canyon

"Don't do it buddy!" he yelled. "Get out of here!"

I had been tricked. The BNSF units had been added in allied force merely to push the UP train over the hill. Everyone—both UP and BNSF—in cahoots. There was no way I could be believed just a railfan. I turned and caught-off the DPU unsteadily, eating shit on the rocks, and when I stood up and turned I saw the white SUV driving back like mad on the other side of train, dirt-road dust swirling up behind it. As the last of the DPUs passed, leaving nothing between me and the approaching SUV, I without hesitation leapt off the steep ravine of thin pines like I would a sand dune and scrambled down a hill thick with decomposing needles and cones to another steep hill where I hit the dirt and laid on my stomach looking back up at the tracks. I heard a radio squalk, and soon a worker stepped forward to look out over the ravine (I think it might have been only a worker because of his bright neon-green vest). He stood with a satisfied air, like I had just plummeted to my death, obviously aware I was no longer on the train, and thankfully not having the incentive to come after me, at least not right then.

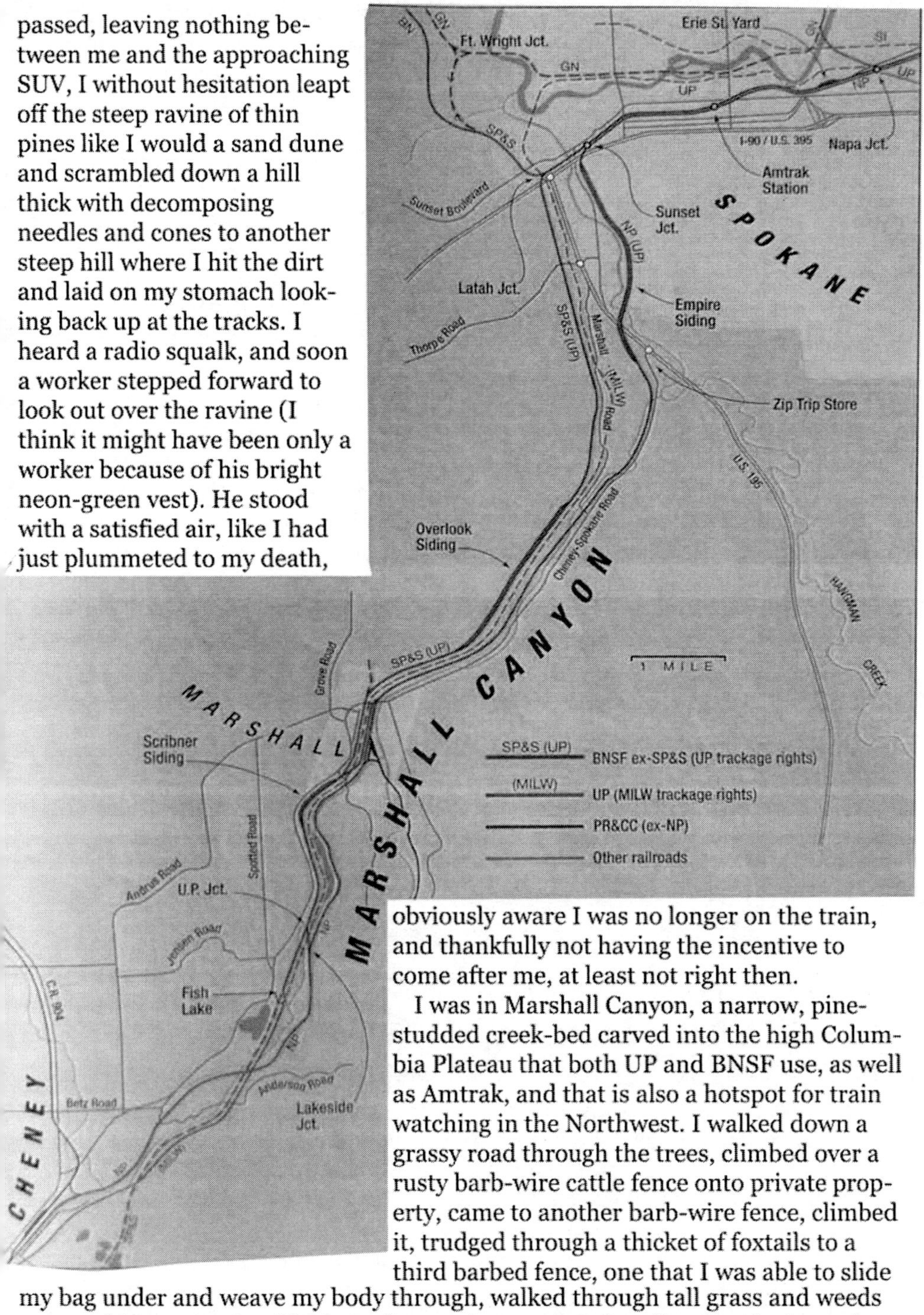

I was in Marshall Canyon, a narrow, pine-studded creek-bed carved into the high Columbia Plateau that both UP and BNSF use, as well as Amtrak, and that is also a hotspot for train watching in the Northwest. I walked down a grassy road through the trees, climbed over a rusty barb-wire cattle fence onto private property, came to another barb-wire fence, climbed it, trudged through a thicket of foxtails to a third barbed fence, one that I was able to slide my bag under and weave my body through, walked through tall grass and weeds to a muddy stream that I had to take my shoes and socks off and wade through, into prickly bushes and thorns and more tall grass and another barbed fence that I lifted my bags over and then climbed over unsteadily to reach the Spokane/Cheney Hwy on the far outskirts of the city. Behind me I could hear a train coming back- the BNSF units—job now done—had detached and were returning to Spokane. I walked maybe ten minutes with my thumb not very seriously out before a nice blue car stopped to pick me up. Inside drove a pipe-smoking, Jewish-looking old man, very genial and very much a do-good-for-others-and-they-in-turn-will-do-good-for-others kind of person who owns a ranch outside of town and refers to Spokane as Redneck Central. He dropped me off at the Amtrak station downtown where I cleaned up and called Whisky to warn them. They were still on the train at Overlook, the siding where I had to bail off, and were both lying on top of the train car opposite the road, hiding from the white SUV that was still prowling the line. Since *I* knew that the *Worker* knew I was no longer on the train, I thought they would be ok (assuming the Worker did not know others were on the train), and I told them to hold tight and they would make it to Hinkle by nightfall.

*

Spokane, WA 1620- This shit hole just keeps getting worse. Yesterday we failed to catch a train and my friend was held at gunpoint and nearly arrested, today *I* got chased off a train out in the boonies, separated from my cohort, and have now just been physically—if not violently—removed from the downtown Amtrak station. I had simply walked up the spiral Greyhound-bus driveway and crossed a track to the platform, a secluded, quiet place in the middle of Spokane where I sat reading, watching trains, and considering my options. After an hour or two some bored janitor in a neon safety vest informed me that I could not wait up top until the station opened later that night. And because I was not supposed to be there he demanded I exit the premises *his* way, through the upstairs lobby, down the steps, and out the station's front door, instead of just letting me cross the one track and exit the way I had come in. A verbal confrontation ensued when I tried to walk past him to do that and he stepped in front of me and got up in my face. I told him to step back and to go wash some toilets and to do his job and quit telling me what to do, and he said he was doing his job and grabbed my backpack and began pulling me away from the tracks. I swatted his hand off and confronted him, but looking at his face I cautioned myself, remembering all the trouble there had already been in Spoken, and in that moment he snatched my glasses from my face and stormed off into the building like a child. I was now unable to see and really not able to do much of anything as he walked away, and I just bit my tongue and followed him into the building and outside to the street where he threw my glasses on the sidewalk, officially kicking me off the premises. I just stood there, incensed, and told him what a miserable fucking person he must be to treat others this way and that he must really hate his miserable job in white-bred Spokane. I

Amtrak station- Spokane

was now back on Sprague Avenue, totally fucking dejected and just wanting to disappear, and at the same time doubly paranoid he was going to call the police (which I wouldn't put past that buster) and that I would be easy to recognize by description and that possibly the incident could then be related to the description that fit the Trespasser who got chased off a train earlier in the day, which may or may not have been reported. I did not need any more trouble in Spokane and so I walked under the first overpass I came to and sat down beside the tracks in pretty much bruising defeat . . . *Now I just want to absolve myself from that whole useless interfacing and get the fuck out of Spokane once and for all . . .*

Chew Chew, a kid I met hopping trains in Eugene last year, who let me photograph his gnarled, torn earlobe, had recent tags on the pillar of the bridge where I sat, which brought me a bit of comfort, and in a sudden turn of luck, not five minutes after sitting down, a BNSF freight came through bearing three units and a conductor leaning out the window and waving jovially in my direction—a welcome contrast from the rest of Spokane. Perhaps the conductor realized I needed a picking-up in more ways than one because it just so happened that the train stopped directly in front of me, presenting itself as a bonafide ride out. It consisted mostly of mixed grainers and hoppers and I did not care where it was going—suicide or not, I was climbing on. I took to a maroon hopper with a high ledge and placed myself down amongst the gaskets and pipes on its back porch, put on my black hoodie and removed my blue hat (I earned a suspicion that it gives me away by standing out, and is, at least on this trip, bad luck), and hunkered down as the train pulled west of town . . . *The train bypasses the first southbound split and continues west, and I don't really care if I'm going back to where I came from . . . but now, in an utterly surprising twist, veers south onto the higher elevated southbound spur at Latah Junction, the same arching offshoot I rode across earlier in the day to bad ends and that I thought belonged to Union Pacific, but apparently BNSF uses as well . . . Heading back up that steep, creaky grade of track into Marshall Canyon, overlooking the same steep ravine across the creek to where BNSF's mainline track is active . . . I am increasingly scared—374-mile marker—as to who's still up here and what's going on . . . (are they still looking for me, waiting for me to come back through?) . . . Overlook—the place of all earlier commotion . . . chugging slowly up the grade be-*

Ewok
Speedy
on the Santa Fe
4-1-08
UNDER
NEW
OWNERSHI
The Iron Pelican
NOT THEIR FAVORITE CUSTOMERS
MISSOULA, MT.
Ewok
Ewok
12-31-06 BC
ONE FOR M.C....
TEX GOTH '10
MUD UP
11-90"
1999
TORCH
TEMPLE, TX
'05
Hom
03
DCH
Bend Over
1 Ore
1898
JOHN
EASLEY 95
Whitefish, MT
7-23-07

Spokane, WA

Latah Junction

tween slants of hillside where trees grow out perpendicular then shoot up toward the sky in L shapes—373-mile marker . . . No signs of other vehicles yet... Staying on the mainline past the very spot where I bailed off earlier . . . The train now slightly on a decline and picking up speed . . . A sigh of relief at the siding's end . . .

The train stopped several miles past Overlook alongside Queen Lucas Lake, a small little stretch of water in between the mainlines of two separate railroads. I walked carefully back to a gondola, climbed up and in and unfortunately found it to be loaded with gnarls of rusty metal scraps. But I rode it anyway, past Scribner and through UP Junction where the train took back to BNSF trackage. Continuing down through Cheney, I peered out from behind the gondola's wall through little holes and saw silos and trains that I recognized from earlier in the day in Spokane.

Overlapping UP

Thirty-miles southwest of Spokane at a siding called Fishtrap—2,300-feet elevation—the train stopped in the middle of nowhere on the Columbia Plateau and I climbed off and looked infinite-miles down the mainline in both directions. I heard a whistle blaring to the south and walked the line back north until I could see the oncoming train's headlights in the distance. I climbed over the line to a field of high grass, continued walking until the northbound passed fervently by, and came to a group of stout, gray MRL hoppers, a particular stock of train I have never before ridden. I found a suitable porch to load up on, but waited off the train until another northbound passed. My train then aired up and I climbed back on as it rolled off along the straightaway . . . *picking up speed fast . . . A small lake passes to the east of the train as major undulations appear in the landscape . . .*

This is the Scablands: a high lava-plain of erratic coulees, heavily eroded soil, and exposed basalt that leaves to the imagination as to how it all became... so scarred. Without a geologic background to serve as context to process this place, the Scablands may appear no more less-ordinary than the rest of the steppe in Eastern Washington. However, it is drastically different, and it took the imagination of one J Harlen Bretz, renegade geologist, to propose a groundbreaking geologic discovery: that at the end of the last ice age great floods deluged the Pacific Northwest creating enormous channelways and waterfalls that were then left empty and dry after the thaw.

The Missoula Floods, the same phenomenal processes that gouged the stunning Deschutes River Canyon (see *Railroad Semantics #2*), that carved the Columbia

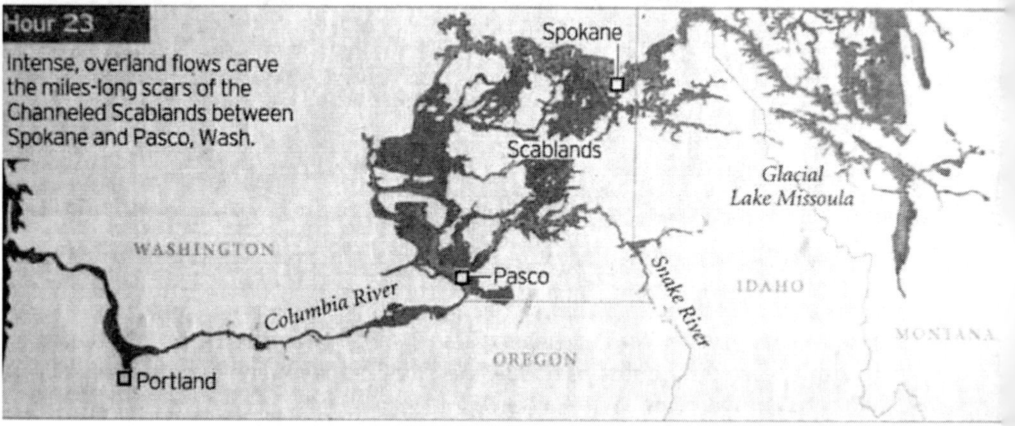

River Gorge through the Cascades Mountains, and that created the rich and fertile Willamette Valley, before all that washed over this plateau of Eastern Washington, eroding the land and exposing its core basalt. Though the Scablands does boast grandiose features (like Dry Falls, Grand Coulee, and Devil's Canyon), it's no Grand Canyon in the sense that riding across it on a freight train doing thirty, forty, fifty miles-per-hour, it makes difficult to appreciate the complexity and notice any dynamism, much like if you were to view a Crop Circle from eye-level with the crops it would appear not *that* out-of-the-ordinary, at first. But if you were to view this landscape from a giant's perspective, from the air or in orbit, you would begin to see it as Bretz saw it—unconventional for a desert, looking rippled like the bottom of a lightly ebbing lakebed, like it was all very much once under water.

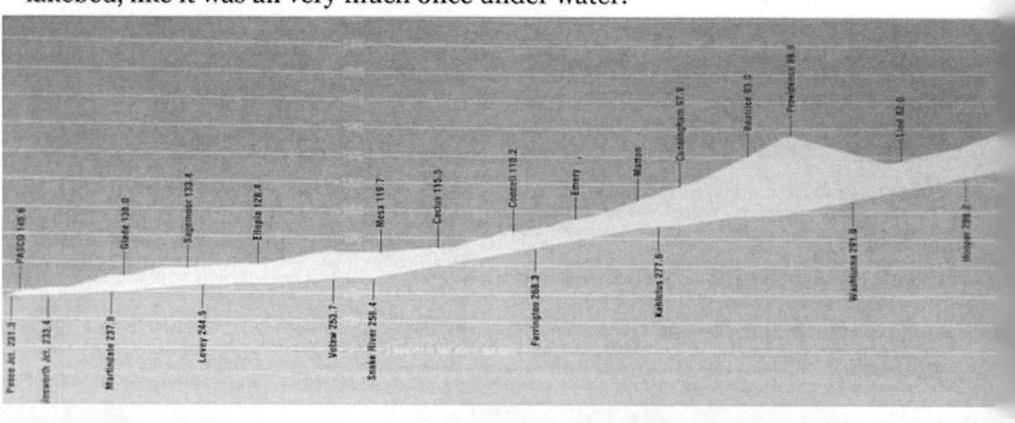

approaching the old Milwaukee Road viaduct remnants

Ritzville, a two-story town . . . *spur tracks, a grain silo, trailers, corrugated-metal buildings, a steeple, abandoned-building foundations, several crossings, loading docks, more corrugated-metal buildings, company buildings and industries, square white houses on estates high up on a bluff, farm machinery, a windmill, a couple of gas stations, a barn, Texaco, a café, and hints of hills all around . . .* Named after farmer and homesteader Phil Ritz who traveled around the region in the early 1900s recruiting people to live here, Ritzville is one of the few remaining towns along BNSF's Lakeside subdivision. Twenty miles south, just past Lind (if there's a town I didn't notice it), the old Milwaukee, St. Paul & Pacific Railroad once bisected this sub, crossing over the tracks on a massive viaduct that looked like it was built to survive the great floods. Now all that's left are huge pillars that hold nothing but were once the supports for that bridge. I could see them far off on the horizon, approaching like the ruins of some ancient Roman architecture. Sand and Beatrice, two joint sidings a few miles later, wrap around the scabbed land in near-constant 6-degree curvature, exposing both the front and rear of the train at the same time as it snakes widely through the hills . . . *The sun falls lower in the sky, sharply illuminating the hills, and basalt formations begin to appear along the tracks, eroded and exposed and imbedded in Palouse hills not as stripped down as the Deschutes River Canyon but still clearly eroded by the same floods . . .*

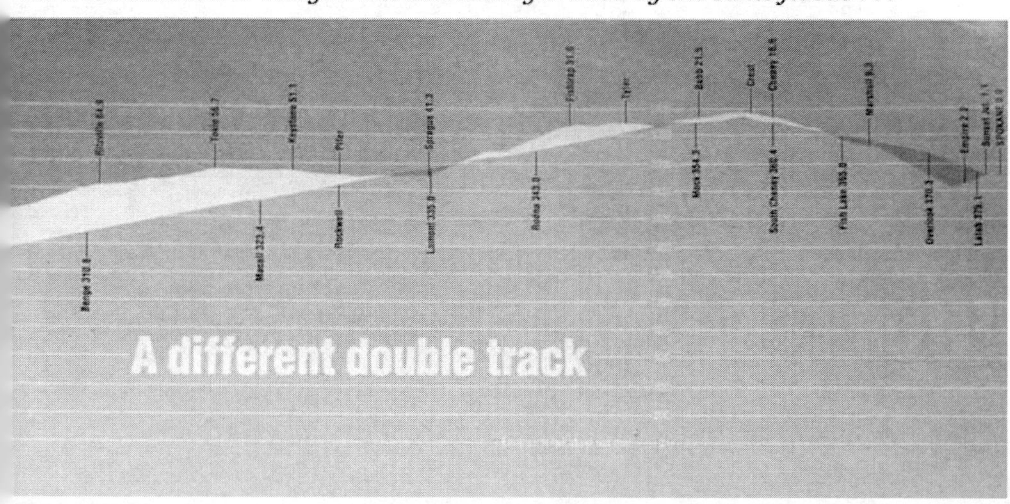

Sand, WA

Beatrice, WA

July 2011

Pasco, WA 0859- Pasco is easily one of the largest yards I have ever been to—terrifyingly confusing at first, sprawling on the outskirts of the flickering Tri-City lights in a desolate expanse of arable desert with no refuge for water. It is comparable to Hinkle, only with a nearby road. The far north Departure-Tracks-looking end where I got off the train waxed dark and empty, and as a doublestack blew furiously north on the mainline, I hopped over to an adjacent line of trains that had begun to move south. I thought I had seen a Freddy on it when I pulled in, and it was now rolling with a DPU so I caught on a Cadillac-grainer porch feeling surprised at my luck. I stuck with the train as it moved incrementally toward the yard, but what I came to realize (and I should of hopped off when I had the chance) was that the line was going up the hump and that that DPU really wasn't a DPU at all (though it had no blinking yellow light signifying it as a yard-unit), but a remote controlled slave-engine slowly pushing the line up a brightly-lit incline to be humped into the yard's bowl. By the time I realized this for certain it would've been too much of a risk to climb off into the highly-lit area, and so I had no choice but to put my things in a cubbyhole on the adjacent back porch, cross over, and hide there like a leper. I could hear that lonely, screeching whine the rails make only when a lone boxcar or two is let fly and drifting perilously slow and frighteningly powerful on momentum only through the bowels of the yard destined for a slow-motion high-impact collision. Things suddenly became bright all around and I could hear the Yardmaster giving instructions on a loud intercom saying, "One more car and then a slight pause," or something like that. Peeking out of the cubbyhole I saw a worker standing over the coupler doing whatever he does to release the coupler and

headin' up the hump

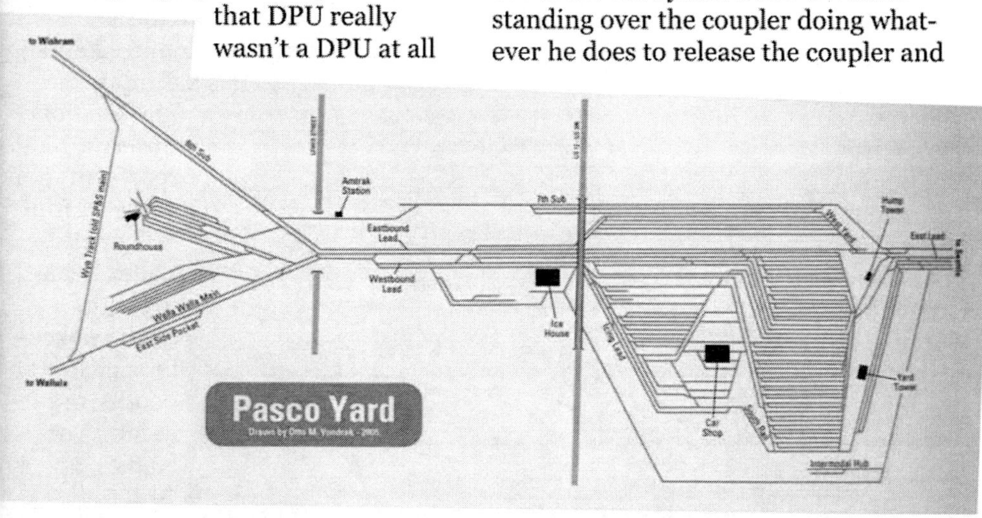

send the hopper rolling down the hump. And I was let fly. I looked back and saw the yard tower and controls and switches and signal board of lights as the train accelerated furiously in freefall, and in my head I remembered hearing stories of cracked skulls and tramps being knocked out cold from collisions—knowingly even—after being sent down the hump. I lay curled in a fetal position with my bag under my head as a pillow shielding me against the solid steel of the train's inner cavity, fearing the serious momentum the hopper was achieving. But thank God for the retarders. I soon felt them squeezing to work, slowing the hopper as I clung anxiously to my position...

A yard since the 1880s, Pasco became Northern Pacific's first hump yard in 1955. It was then extensively modified in the early 1970s, and since the reopening of Stampede Pass has become BNSF's main hump yard in the Pacific Northwest with 47 classification tracks.

There's really no way to anticipate the impact. I could not have risked climbing off in the face of something so sudden and so severe, and so I just had to ride through the crash, and it came so forcefully that the ten-ton train car stopped dead from the inelastic-collision as if it had hit a stone wall, heaving my entire body forward in a vicious jolt of impetus, the deafening noise and ringing steel causing my head to immediately ache. But I survived...

I quickly climbed off before anything else could hit and carefully worked my way out of the bowl back to the west side of the yard toward the mainline, and I continued walking south in the shadows looking for a source of hydration. I walked for miles along scattered lines of trains to an overpass, past which is a large loading-dock area behind an abandoned factory abutting the tracks. From there I could see a gas station of some sort glowing from behind several backyards across a street. I slept on that loading-dock platform, which was nice because I was off the ground (though not on a rooftop or anything). I slept well into the early morning sun and caught the first thing coming through—a loaded coal train moving slowly (unlike everything else). I waited patiently and eventually caught onto the DPU.

July 2011

Salem, OR 1000- The Saturday Market in Salem occupies a large parking lot downtown off Center Street and is less commercialized than Portland's Old Town/ Skidmore Fountain tourist extravaganza where the same burnt out old buskers wax like radically new to the hip urban crowd and the same greasy sheisters peddle their cheap curios to susceptible newcomers like a magi paradise, and not as anarchic as Eugene's utterly weird Country Fairish market, but is, Salem's Saturday Market, nonetheless a good representation of the fruitful Willamette Valley, teeming with fresh-cooked-breakfast booths, organic-farm vegetables, and a

boxcar in Salem

good array of old-biddy crafts. It's a beautiful morning in Salem, fresh and clear like the Oregon spring, and hot... it's going to be.

Salem always makes me think of *Emperor of the North*, perhaps because of its more traditional and less transient demographic, but also because it just has a slower pace and an old-time feel to it. Trains run right through the middle of town, roaring past sub-college campuses and courthouses, literally bisecting the city; pathways cut through the woods to lazy streams where you'll likely find jungles (and issued vagrancy tickets), places where you can easily wait in the shade; and the rickety old yard never holds more than a handful of cars and always seems to be asleep. Grass grows up tall between the tracks and all along the edges, glistening in the dew. This morning, one look outside the boxcar and I knew right where I was.

southbound: Portland, OR

I had caught the train as it came rolling past Steel Bridge early this morning in Portland. Multiple units veered a general manifest southeast toward Brooklyn yard and I didn't think too much about whether it was going all the way or not. I just woke up, saw an empty boxcar approaching, and literally rolled off the pillar I slept atop. I threw my stuff in on the run, jumped inside, and fell right back asleep as the train rumbled south.

At the crack of dawn the train stopped for an hour or so at a siding north of Salem (probably Gervais) and eventually a northbound, the morning Cascades, passed. An hour or so later the train stopped again and cut its air. I had slept on a wretchedly rusty floor, I saw upon waking, and so I threw my stuff out onto the grass to pack it up. The boxcar I had ridden in turned out to be an old AERC (Albany Eastern Railway Company), which serves the likes of Albany Oregon's shortlines and is common in off-the-beatin'-path towns like Lebanon and Sweet Home but is rarely seen as far south as Eugene. The whole line was short enough to fit entirely in the Salem yard and a string of gondolas on the back of the line hinted at Willamette and Pacific (I know how the W&P line west to Toledo favors gondolas. I can tell by the many Wild Man monikers I've seen dated with locations along that line and because I accidentally caught-out of Albany on a line of empty gondolas years ago that took me miles west before I caught back off and had to walk back to town). Adding all of this up, I had no doubt that the line was going only as far as Albany, and so I got off to enjoy the Salem sunshine.

*

Yesterday, Pasco proved to be a difficult place to catch-out, mainly because I didn't know of a good place to catch a train, nor did I know how to tell if one was even going the direction I wanted of what that direction entailed. Some-

times, and this is what I learned in Spokane, but also in Everett a little bit, and what I wanted to exercise in Pasco, sometimes you got to let the train come to you. You can't always go chasing trains down, trying to catch them on the fly; you've got to put yourself in the best strategic catch-out spot and wait for the train to come to you—that's how it works. However, I did not know the layout of the yard and tracks in Pasco (trains actually depart the yard GEO southbound, then veer west across the Columbia on a low steel trestle before turning back south and then finally west again once hitting the Gorge), and right away upon waking I caught the DPU on a line of loaded coal-cars thinking that if it were rolling south it could only ultimately be going west (because BNSF does not cross over into Oregon this far east was my reasoning, but I again hadn't done my research). So I stayed on, surprised again at my luck as it rolled past the Amtrak station into an area of eight departure tracks holding four long lines bordering the NF Lampson Crane Company. The train sat idle for an hour and I read, but I eventually decided not to nerve-rackingly wait in the DPU and have to keep an eye out in two directions at all times, and so I walked over to another line and found an open boxcar close enough to the coal train that I could run back over to it if it departed.

There was no activity all morning, and as the high, afternoon sun arced westward in the blue orb sky, cutting into the boxcar through the ajar west-facing door, the train car began to warm (as a good conductor of heat will). My CC guide does place emphasis on the west side of the yard (as in SW), mentioning a "catch-out bridge" for westbounds, which sounded about right, and with a zoom lens on my camera I took a 200mm photo and then zoomed in on the zoomed-photo to barely make out in the far, far distance south, down past the front units of the entire mile-long coal train, a bridge structure—the Catch-Out Bridge—and so I decided to hike it down there and wait, thinking westbounds possibly come off another branch of the mainline and pass through the junction there (heading GEO southbound but eventually west). That bridge, at Ainsworth Junction, dates back to the nascence of the Pasco yard and crosses the Snake River at its confluence with the Columbia. It was a much further walk than what it appeared to be and by the time I reached the bridge I could see that it was one of those old-fashioned drawbridges that stays up for boats and comes down for occasional trains to pass. There was not an

catch-out bridge

illegal mark on the bridge save for some really bad gang-tags graffitied in cheap spray paint held in an amateur, far-from-the-surface way. It was obviously not a good waiting spot for trains. I knew that with the amount of freight traffic coming into the enormous Pasco hump-yard the bridge would have to like always be down to account for train capacity, unless ships didn't use the channel any more at all, but that obviously was not the case because the bridge was up, as in a raised position. Where these tracks went I did not know; it could be UP's line to Hinkle for all I know (which is where Whisky and Aware made it to last night on the train that I got flushed off of. They survived (A) by not being lazy and getting themselves spotted, like me, and (B), after stashing their bags entirely out of sight in the cubby-hole, hiding on top of the train from the white SUV driving up and down the line. They said the train remained at Overlook for upwards of five hours before continuing on south, which must've been one hell of a nerve-racking time!).

Snake River/Columbia-confluence

If a train had come I probably would have caught it, but I soon bit the reality-bullet and retraced my steps away from Ainsworth Junction back to the road (also called Ainsworth) and I hiked a good couple of miles alongside the crane factory, all the way back to downtown Pasco, which might as well be on another planet from Spokane, being largely Hispanic—a migrant-worker community with lots of *'eritas*, Mexican markets, night-club posters advertising sexy mamacitas and stoic-looking Mariachi bands, and plenty of auto-part shops and taco carts. Pacso is, after all, South American in spirit, as it is named after the Andes mountain-town Cerro del Pasco, in Peru. The story goes that in the 1880s when Northern Pacific founded Pasco as a stop between Portland and Spokane, Virgil Bogue, an engineer for the railroad that had just come from an idyllic, high-elevation-climated place in Peru where he had helped build a railroad, became so aggravated by the Columbia Plateau's low-elevation, humid summer hottage that he sarcastically named the town after where he wished he still was, and it stuck.

I asked several people in Pasco if they could tell me where the Amtrak station was, but *no hablar Englise*. I eventually found it on my own at the end of Tacoma St. bordering the south end of the yard. After washing up I sat down to eat some comeda just as a thundering northbound came through on the closest-in line. Minutes later a three-unit GM began to pull out from the yard and I packed up my shit and headed outside just in case. I told myself that if the train started to

bridge over Columbia River

veer west that I'd catch it, and it did, so I walked into the open expanse in front of the Amtrak station and in broad daylight caught-on the only (semi)ridable that far back on the line—a suicide porch on the back of a hopper that was rolling at a faster-than-I-could-run pace, and quickening. Soon I crossed the Columbia River on a long, low-lying bridge. The train pulled onto Hover, the very first siding, to let pass a northbound GM of quaking velocity, and here, directly underneath another-set-of-track's bridge (Postkid Blues up on the side), I walked the line up to the only other ridable I had seen, a big-belly Canadian grainer with cow pie-like flaxseed mudcaking the porch. The train soon departed Hover, picked up speed through the sun-bleached Palouse Loess, and veered west along the north bank of the Columbia River Gorge . . . *Washington is almost completely in shadow as Oregon remains sunlit beautifully . . . Coming up on a bridge of some sort . . . an orchard down below—beautiful property . . . A farmhouse, a couple of horses, all these trees green and lush—mile 115—a bridge ahead, windmills on the Washington side high above, Mt. Hood enormous in the distance looking just like it does on a Henry Weinhardt's bottle . . . A grape vineyard right on the Gorge here . . . and rows of trees—Maryhill . . . On the mainline at Maryhill siding . . . (Just before the bridge that crosses the Columbia, on a bridge that crosses the tracks and the road, there is an old Coaltrain on the pillars and I wish to God I could have gotten a picture) . . . People all along the Washington riverbank fishing . . . eddies on the surface of the water . . . Shadows begin to emerge on the Oregon landscape . . . White pickup-trucks and dogs running*

Mt. Hood on the Columbia River Gorge

around . . . orchards in the valley . . . tree farms galore . . . islands of lava rock out in the middle of the river . . . craggy pillars north of the train line . . . Screeching through blasted-out walls of rock warped by floods . . . Eroded structures . . . The train wraps around the land in an S . . . wire fences protect against falling boulders . . . Columns and columns of basalt rock . . . Birds fly to their nests on vertical structures . . . Islands of lava rock in the Columbia River . . . fishing planks . . . A deer lies dead on the gravel path beside the tracks . . . Air warm, sky a perfect pastel blue . . . The first tunnel, only about fifty-feet, exits me into the sun shining right on my face . . . Just past where the Deschutes River opens up in Oregon . . . Passing through Wishram—Columbia River Bridge (Fallbridge) up ahead . . . Four-tracks wide and nothing laid up except for way down there are a few cars . . . Not slowing down one bit as the yard widens to eight tracks plus the mainline . . . Tiny huts and houses whiz by north of the train . . . Barreling through Wishram . . . An old Northern Pacific steam engine encaged in a fence on the property . . . Amtrak station . . . As the yard ends the train loses a little momentum but stays on the northernmost track, not the least bit interested in crossing Fallbridge to Oregon and entirely focused on continuing west to Vancouver . . . as the sun sets . . . A brief tunnel that is nothing, then a second, third, fourth, and fifth, which all run right through the basalt

Wishram yard

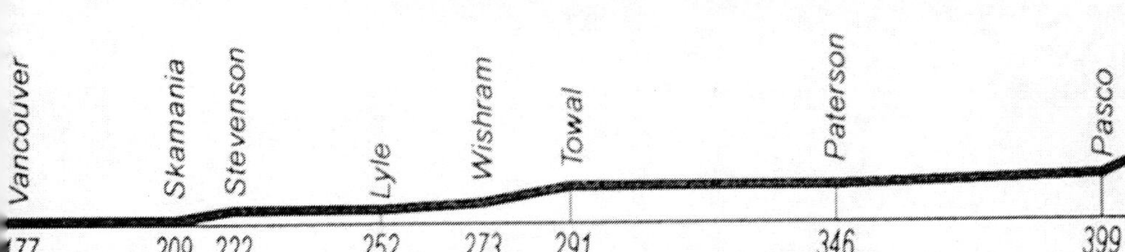

Columbia River Gorge- Washington

Columbia River Gorge- Washington

RailroadSemantics.com
RailroadSemantics@hotmail.com

www.Microcosm.Pub
SKILLS TO CHANGE YOUR LIFE AND THE WORLD
2752 N WILLIAMS AVE • PORTLAND, OR 97227

$7.95 U.S. / $9.99 CANADA

ISBN 978-1-62106-843-3
US$7.95